Impossible Choices

A Mother's Struggle to Save Her Daughters

Leni Goodman
with contributions by Cache Goodman

Praise for *Impossible Choices*

Making impossible choices is often at the heart of our human fate. Stubborn, dedicated, refusing to stay within the lines, Leni Goodman creates a world that lives on these pages. Not just for parents, but for all who wonder at the strength of the human heart.
—JOAN NESTLE, co-founder of The Lesbian Herstory Archives, activist and author of *A Restricted Country* and *A Fragile Union*

Mesmerizing! "*Impossible Choices*" is a magnificent story of triumph over tragedy. An inspirational memoir detailing a mother's love so fierce it challenges my own understanding of parenting and loss.
—STEPHANIE SCHROEDER, author of *Beautiful Wreck, Sex Lies and Suicide*

An inspiring story of love and determination told with wonderful real writing. An important book for parents to share with their children.
—DOREEN RAPPAPORT, author of *Beyond Courage* (The Untold Story of Jewish Resistance during The Holocaust)

I was deeply moved by this mother's quiet heroism as she never gave up in her struggle to find ways to save her children…will arouse passionate interest in a wide range of readers.
—NAOMI RAPLANSKY, poet, author of *Collected Poems*

Engrossing, honest and moving writing with the sense of destiny one finds in Greek tragedy. ….awaking a deep response in its readers as they follow the writer's struggles to make the "right" choices for her daughters.
—EVA KOLLISCH, author of *The Ground Under My Feet* and *Girl in Movement*

Leni Goodman has a powerful story to tell, and she tells it with intelligence, insight and grace. Her story deserves a wide readership.
—ANN BANNON, author of *Beebo Brinker*

Impossible Choices

A Mother's Struggle to Save Her Daughters

IN THE MIDST OF WINTER
I DISCOVERED IN ME AN INDOMINABLE SUMMER
Albert Camus

This is a true story, although some names and details have been changed.

ISBN: 1494294443
ISBN 13: 9781494294441
Library of Congress Control Number: 2013921954
CreateSpace Independent Publishing Platform
North Charleston, South Carolina

To Joan, the best sister in the world and the most incredible aunt to Julie and Cache

Prologue

I was relaxing on Julie's bench in Riverside Park, reading in the warm late afternoon sun. Whenever I looked up, I saw the catalpa tree we had planted between two large oaks on the grassy expanse in front of me. Her tree was finally bursting with green leaves after its winter barrenness, and newly formed delicate white flower pods were beginning to open, as they did for a few weeks each June

I noticed children and parents bearing gifts gathering near two tables under one of the oak trees. I stopped reading as I began to hear music from a CD player.

There once was an ugly duckling with feathers all stubby and brown
And the other birds in so many words
Said…get out of town

I was transported back to late December 1972. Julie was almost six years old. We were in the playroom on the children's floor in New York Hospital. There were other children there, a few with their parents and some sitting around a table drawing with the recreation therapist. Julie was wearing a green hospital gown with the white from her undies peeking out as she climbed onto a platform in the center of the playroom, gathering blocks from a box as she went along. The left side of her head was shaved and bandaged and the other half had shoulder length shiny brown hair. The playroom phonograph was playing.

And he went with a quack and a waddle and a quack
And a flurry of eider down

She stopped climbing, jumped down from the platform, and ran to me. I was sitting on a small chair off to the side under the large sun filled windows, trying to concentrate on what the social worker was saying. Julie interrupted her, wanting me, needing me closer to the platform so I could watch her performance. I happily gave in. That talk could wait, I thought. Having captured her audience, Julie climbed back onto the platform and transformed herself into a baby bird, flapping her elbows, hip-hopping back and forth along the platform edge.

That poor little ugly duckling went wandering far and near
At every place they said to his face
Now get out of here
And he went with a quack and a waddle and a quack and a very
Unhappy tear.

Then she started crawling around the platform, looking for a place to hide. I sat there unable to take my eyes off my daughter. I felt the social worker watching me as she too took in Julie's performance. We had met a few days before and it was going to be her job to help me digest the information the doctors had just given me. She was so young, I thought. How could she even begin to understand what I was going through? How could she be able to help me cope? The tumor had already metastasized, and my performing duckling up on that platform had only six months to live.

All through the wintertime he hid himself away
Ashamed to show his face, afraid of what others might say

My husband and I had separated the year before; and I was still feeling fragile. I was a thirty-six-year old, mostly unemployed actress and mother, trying to figure out who I was without the love of my life. And now I was in this surreal nightmare, hoping to wake up. This couldn't be really happening–this only happened in the movies or on the soap operas for which I auditioned.

All through the winter in his lonely clump of weeds
Till a flock of swans spied him there and very soon agreed
You're a very fine swan indeed.

Julie started to unfold from the heap she had rolled herself into and began to blossom into the swan she was, right before my eyes, our eyes–because by this time, her performance had attracted the other children and their parents who were in the playroom. They gathered around the platform, some in wheelchairs, some ambulatory, pulling their medication poles and chairs closer to watch the show.

Swan ... Me? A swan? Go on.
You're a swan. Take a look at yourself in the lake and you'll see
And he looked and he saw and he said
AHHH it's me.... I am a swan.

Julie giggled seeing her audience and started dancing and skipping around the platform. Her blue eyes were shining in the sunlight and her face was happier than I had seen in months. The long hair on the right side of her head was bouncing up and down as the children around the platform clapped in time with her joyous skipping. At that moment, I wanted to forget the social worker sitting next to me. I did not want to think about the next six months

And now, sitting on that bench almost forty years later, I shut my eyes to the party scene unfolding on the grass in front of me and stayed frozen in time with the image of my joyful little swan still dancing.

one

1972 -1974

Julie emerged from her operation to remove the tumor in her brain looking and feeling like her old self, except half her head was completely bald with a large scar. She recovered in the hospital for a few weeks as I slowly realized how little time we had left.

The radiation treatments started her last few days in the hospital, and then we traveled back and forth from home each day to complete the two-week protocol. At the beginning of the second week, her remaining hair fell out in clumps until she was completely bald. I watched her and marveled at how she viewed this as a new adventure. One day a man on the bus said something to me about my son. Julie turned to him and said, "I'm not a boy. I'm a girl. Can't you see my Mary Janes?"

The social worker had given me the address of a wig store, and I asked Julie if she wanted to wear a wig until her hair grew back. With a big smile, she asked if she could get any wig she wanted. When we got to the store, I began picking out light brown wigs with bangs that recreated her original hair style and color. She tried on each one, looked in the mirror and with a shrug pulled it off and handed it back to me. Suddenly, her eyes lit up as she pointed to a long blonde curly wig and asked the saleslady if she could try it on. When she looked in the mirror she said, "This is the one I want. I want to look like Cinderella." I saw the smile on her face and was sold. Cinderella and I walked out of the store holding hands.

When she went back to school the next week, she got varying comments on her new look. Some kids liked her better bald, some liked the wig, and some liked it when she wore it inside out. At the Christmas show that year she sang "The Twelve Days of Christmas" and was having such a good time in front of her classmates and their parents that she improvised a thirteenth-day stanza.

"On the thirteenth day of Christmas my true love sent to me a great big bunch of roses and all the presents I ever wanted." Then she triumphantly twirled around twice and bent forward in a deep bow to the applause.

I sat in the audience imprinting this moment in my memory, as I was doing with each moment since her diagnosis. The only way I was able to get through a day was to keep myself present in every moment, and not allow my mind to race ahead and miss a second of our precious time together.

I kept myself busy with my weekly acting class, the jewelry line, and the interviews for the craft book my soon-to-be ex-husband and I had recently written on shells—activities that helped get me through the horror of dealing with the unreal world of hospital visits and doctors appointments. Each day I saw that the social worker was the go-to person for every parent and their child—and for me she had become the one person crucial to my sanity. As I spent time in this new world, I began to feel that my devotion to acting was a frivolous choice.

In the 1970s, one could file for divorce on the grounds of irreconcilable differences by signing a separation agreement and living apart for two years. Stu and I had just passed the two year point, and I was now able to move ahead with our divorce.

My sister, Joan, who was five years younger than I, had followed in my mother's footsteps and become a lawyer. Although she was working as an entertainment attorney at Madison Square Garden and had not handled a divorce case yet, she had been able to draft the separation papers to begin the process. Now that the two years has elapsed, she asked a matrimonial lawyer friend to file the necessary papers and appear with me in court in front of the judge

The morning I went to court, Julie was happily attending school in her blonde Cinderella wig. There was nothing else to do until the tumor gathered strength again and new symptoms appeared showing us where it had gained hold. My lawyer met me outside the courtroom and went over the questions she was going to ask me in front of the judge. I was surprised to feel my knees shaking when I actually had to stand up in court, state my name, and swear on a Bible to tell the truth, the whole truth, and nothing but the truth

My sister invited me to meet her after my appearance in court at La Grenouille, an elegant four-star French restaurant in the East fifties. I had never eaten at a four-star restaurant and was looking forward to the experience. When I arrived, she was already there. I was led back past huge overflowing vases of flowers to where she was sitting in a large raised banquette along the side of the ornately furnished dining room. I slid in next to her, still shaking a bit from my courtroom experience. We first ordered a glass of wine to celebrate my new beginning and then set to the task of trying to decipher the elaborate menu written completely in French.

On the day I officially started my new life as a single mom, my dear sister was treating me to a lavish three course French luncheon. Neither of us knowing what lay ahead.

Julie's hair began to grow back although the new fuzzy growth was a bit darker brown than before with fewer blonde highlights. She still wore her Cinderella wig most days, but I could see a time in the next few months when her own hair would be long enough for her to put away the wig.

My sister's years at Madison Square Garden were golden years for all of us, especially Julie, her own special niece. Thanks to Aunt Joan, she had her choice of any and every item in the Garden's gift shop storeroom, as well as front row tickets to every event she wanted. When Julie was six, I took her to Radio City Music Hall to see the film *Auntie Mame*, and she immediately renamed Aunt Joan as Auntie Mame, and herself Patrick.

When the circus came to town, Joan arranged for her to meet her favorite animal trainer, Gunther Gabel Williams, and had her picture taken with him.

She also arranged to have Julie chosen as one of the children in the beginning parade around the arena with all the animals and clowns and stars. I could see from the stands, Julie, in her blonde wig, beaming with pride as she circled the arena with a small group of other kids amid the acrobats waving to the crowd. After she had been whisked down to the arena, I tried to block out a father complaining that his son wasn't picked, as the staff person explained they had to let the girl who was dying go in his place. A few months later, Julie got to scream in ecstasy with an audience full of preteens as her idol David Cassidy from *The Partridge Family*, sang just a few rows in front of her in his skin-tight, white cowboy outfit.

Over her Christmas vacation we went to Puerto Rico to stay at the condo of one of my friends for a week. I packed up Julie and our little dog Dorie and made my first airplane trip as a divorced woman. We spent our days on the beach or around the pool at his apartment building. The warm sun felt healing, and now, after seven months free from hospitals and doctors offices, I had stopped waiting for the other shoe to drop and was getting used to enjoying life with my child. Toward the end of our trip, I was sitting at a table near the pool having a snack. When Julie got hungry she jumped out of the pool and ran over to me. As she approached, she started laughing. "Mommy that's a magic table. The food is floating on top of it." It took me a while to figure out she could see the basket of chicken but not the table around it. My stomach clutched. I knew this was not good. Over the next few days, she mentioned other missing parts of objects. I couldn't wait for our flight home to find out what was going on.

In the cab on the way home from the airport, I called her doctor, and he asked me to bring her in the next day. After he examined her, he quietly said "She's losing her peripheral vision. Now you have to decide what further treatment you want to pursue to stop this new tumor growth." He described the two most promising options. One was a new and mostly untried chemo treatment in the state of Washington, the other a more tried chemo combination that could be done at Memorial Sloan-Kettering, here in New York. Neither one promised a cure, just the possibility of more time.

I didn't want Julie to be a guinea pig, and I was reluctant to move us far from home, so I made the decision to go with the chemo treatment at Sloan-Kettering. Julie continued going to school between the outpatient treatments, which took one day every two weeks. We soon got into a routine of going to the hospital, Julie throwing up on the way home, resting for two days, going back to school for the next two weeks and then starting the procedure over again.

One night when I was putting her to sleep, after I had finished singing her good- night songs, she told me about her imaginary friends who kept her company. On the wall opposite her bed she imagined bunk beds for all the lost boys and Peter. She said they also accompanied her to the hospital for her treatments along with all her classmates from school.

I began to make friends with the parents and children we met each week at the outpatient clinic. Many of the children were Julie's age and older, but some were much younger. There was one little boy who cried each time the doctor wanted to take blood from his finger. Julie would get upset when he began to cry. One week, she went up to the doctor and offered her finger for him to take blood from instead of the little boy's. The doctor let her come into the room with them and she held the boy's hand and talked to him during the procedure. He always ran up to her to hold his hand after that.

I kept taking her for chemo every two weeks for most of the next year, because I didn't know what else to do. I tried to pretend that she would get better, even though I had been told that this was only a holding pattern; the chemo just kept the malignant cells off balance and unable to form a group response for a while, but in the end there was nothing that could stop them.

To this day, I still ask myself why I kept letting them pour that poison into her veins until that last treatment, after which I watched her over twenty-four hours slowly lose her ability to talk or move more than her left leg up and down a bit. But she did understand everything I said and would make ahhh sounds of agreement or crying sounds of upset when I spoke to her. Leukoencephalopathy was the name for what the chemo did to her brain. That's when they stopped, shrugged their shoulders, and, when the tumor did not reappear, said, "The treatments were a success. This is the first time someone with this type of tumor lived." It didn't matter to them in what condition she was. She was alive, and that was considered good medicine.

two

Abandon all hope ye who enter here

Dante Alighieri

Stu came with me when I brought her into the emergency the night that last chemo treatment poisoned her system. This time it was the children's ward at Memorial Sloan- Kettering. He stayed with her as she was being admitted, while I went home for a change of clothes. He also visited her during her stay. She loved seeing him, giggling whenever he peeked in at her door. But I felt so disconnected from him at this point that I couldn't seek any comfort from his presence; nor was he able to offer any help with the various decisions I was being asked to make.

My days were spent sitting next to Julie's bed, reading to her, singing, moving her, tickling her, trying in every way to keep in contact with my little girl who was locked up inside her almost unmoving body. I could see in her eyes, which followed me wherever I moved, that she understood what I was saying. She'd respond appropriately by making ahh sounds for happiness or agreement when I spoke of topics she liked or sang a song she knew, and crying sounds of sadness or anger when I talked about her illness or being in the hospital.

Most nights I'd go home, crawl into bed and try to sleep, but sometimes I'd go to dinner with one of the few friends who could bear being with me as I numbly attempted to make conversation. Since Julie couldn't call for help, I arranged for a private duty nurse each night. So far, the insurance, Stu's insurance, was covering everything, including these nurses. I didn't think anyone could ever use up a million dollars worth of insurance, but we were edging closer each month.

Whenever a new resident rotated through, they would sit me down in a quiet corner and try to convince me to ship Julie off to a nursing home so I could get on with my life. Each resident said the same thing—that taking Julie home was an unhealthy decision. They each thought they would be the one to make me see the light. One resident suggested that I meet with the unit's psychiatrist to help me understand Julie's state of mind. I thought this was a bizarre request, as the staff had already made it clear that they did not think Julie had any viable state of mind. I agreed to meet with him, hoping to enlist an ally in my quest to obtain some cognitive therapy for her. During our session it was clear he was there to analyze me, as he asked no questions about Julie. In fact, when I asked for his input regarding therapy, he said he had not even seen her.

I made every effort to sound sane and rational as we talked, afraid if I sounded unreasonable or hysterical it would be used to get Julie discharged before I had a next step planned. After our session, no one mentioned his visit or his conclusions, even though I asked. One night about a month later, a private duty nurse, who read his notes in the chart, whispered to me with a gleam in her eye, as if she were betraying the hierarchy, that he had written "he'd found no pathology and that I was a caring mother wanting to do the best for my child."

Once a week I left Julie's bedside to go to my acting class with Warren Robertson. I didn't have the emotional energy to commit to working with a partner on a scene, but I was glad to have a reason to leave the unreal world in the hospital, go to class, watch the other students perform and hear Warren's comments. I also looked forward to being called on to do the song-and-dance exercise. This was a signature Actor's Studio exercise to help an actor connect to his or her deep-seated emotions. It is a deceptively simple exercise, requiring only a willingness to stand relaxed in front of the class and sing slowly and as deeply as possible a simple tune like Happy Birthday, or even a series of sounds, making sure that each note resonates and vibrates deep inside.

Each week I crossed my fingers and hoped to be called on for the song-and-dance When Warren finally called my name, I stood up and felt my knees grow weak and that familiar dizziness I'd get when overcome with fear. I climbed the two small steps up to the stage area and took my place center stage, looking straight ahead. I shook my hands and turned my head side to side, trying to relax. Then I heard Warren's gentle deep voice encouraging me to begin my song.

"Haaaaaaapppppeeee birrrrrrrrth daaaaaaaaaa toooooooooo yooooooooo."

I felt the sounds deep in my chest begin to reverberate and release the pain and horror I had been holding down.

As I continued to sing, the words kept vibrating and going deeper. I felt my chest opening wide and releasing more pain with each sound I made. The sounds plunged deeper and I began shaking and sobbing. Tears rolled down my cheeks and colored the sounds as they burst forth from deep inside me and floated out into the air.

When I finished the song I took several deep, relaxing breaths. A fellow student in the first row leaned forward and handed me some tissues. Warren thanked me for my work and I somehow made my way back to my seat. As I settled down I felt more relaxed than I had been in weeks and I felt a deep connection to the other students, even those I did not know well. I turned my attention back to the stage, where two students were setting up to begin their scene.

After a few months Warren began to notice I wasn't bringing in any scenes and asked to meet with me. I told him what was going on and admitted out loud for the first time that I had lost my hunger to act. He suggested I move to his assistant's class, where I would be under less pressure to bring in a scene, and see what happened as time went on. His assistant was a very kind actor and director and allowed me more frequent opportunities to get up for the song-and-dance. I even found myself working on a scene for class at one point. But something was missing. Acting was all that I had ever wanted to do. It was where I felt most alive, where I knew I belonged. And now all those feelings were gone. I didn't know where they had gone and had no idea how to find them again. I continued going to this new class for a few more months until I could bring myself to finally let go of that dream. It was an old dream from a different time and place.

three

1950
In the beginning

It all started when I was a young, very shy child with my mother deciding to take me to drama classes on Saturday morning; and it wound up with me wanting to spend my life on the stage in front of the world. Those Saturday mornings in class, learning how to perform, had transformed me from being so nervous that I threw up every morning on my way to school in the first grade, to entering the talent show in the seventh grade. In the show I performed a monologue as a society woman giving a speech to her garden club and walked off with first prize. My teacher suggested to my parents that I audition for a new high school that combined academics with theatrical training. I auditioned for that school in the fall of my eighth grade.

Performing Arts High School was housed in an old school building on Forty-Sixth Street between Sixth Avenue and Broadway, around the corner from the Palace Theatre, with all of Times Square nearby. The day of my audition, my mother drove me to the subway station on Hillside Avenue, so I wouldn't have to wait for the bus, and then I got on the F train into Manhattan.

I came prepared to perform my garden club monologue and then I was asked to improvise some additional scenes. After I did the scenes, the three teachers who were in the room thanked me and said I would receive a letter in a few weeks. On the long train back to Queens, I began fantasizing about going to school in Manhattan and learning to be a professional actress. Every day I rushed home to check the mail until my letter of acceptance arrived.

Dr. Franklin Keller was the principal and guiding light of PA. I was told that he had been fighting for years with the Board of Education for his vision of a performing arts school. They finally agreed and at first added it onto the School of Maritime Trades. The first classes in the mid forties were held on a ship in the harbor along with the maritime trade students. When Dr.Keller found the deserted school building on West Forty-Sixth St, he was able to talk the Board into the funds to open it, and the High School of Performing Arts was born.

Dr. Keller arranged to meet with each new student, and on my first day of school I was ushered into his office. He was a tall man with grayish-blond hair and steel framed glasses. He greeted me with a big smile as he shook my hand and welcomed me into PA. Then he walked me over to a chair near his desk. As I sat down, I saw on one corner of his enormous desk a porcelain replica of a pair of vibrant red ballet slippers tied together with a matching red ribbon. "Oh my God, I blurted out "I can't believe you have the Red Shoes. That's my favorite movie."

"Mine too," he nodded.

At that moment I knew I was in the right place to begin my journey to become an actress.

four

1954-1963

When I graduated from PA, I was accepted with a partial scholarship into the Theatre program at Syracuse University. But by the end of my first year there, even though the Drama Department was very professional and I was getting parts in the productions, I was worried casting directors in New York would forget me if I stayed away any longer and so I transferred to the School of Dramatic Arts at Columbia University. It was one of the few co-ed schools on campus, and I could take my academics in the college or at Barnard and obtain a BFA in Theatre with a minor in English, as I promised my father I would be prepared to teach if necessary.

I was back in New York and living at home again. In that year I was away, the Korean War ended, Eisenhower was campaigning for his second term as president, with Nixon as his VP. The Civil Rights Movement had motivated the Supreme Court to integrate the schools in Little Rock, and the Twist was the new dance rage, with Bill Haley's "Rock around the Clock" blaring from the radio. And sadly, I had missed my sister's first period and seeing her put on her first garter belt and nylon stockings.

Each summer I went away to stock, first as an apprentice and later as the publicity director, also performing small parts in the star productions that came to our theatre. I was gaining experiences and filling in my resume. In the city I made rounds and took every extra and bit part I was offered in the various TV and films that were being shot here.

The last season in stock, just after I had graduated from Columbia, I met an apprentice from New Mexico who was planning to move to New York to pursue an acting career, and to join her best friend, who was a model. They were going to find an apartment and were interested in another roommate to share the expenses. My father had died the year after I graduated from college and I had not allowed myself to think about leaving my mother so soon after this loss. Nor did I want to leave my younger sister, who just started college, at home with all the responsibility of helping my mother cope, and with caring for our big house. But I could not resist this opportunity. Now at twenty-four years of age, I began to make plans of how I could make the move into the city to start my own life and also be there at home for my mother and sister.

In the fall, in spite of my mother's objections and her admonition to me from the top of our circular staircase that if I moved I would be the cause of her death, I finally moved away from home, to a sublet apartment on West Fifty-Eighth Street with Ivy and her friend, Bennie, who had already begun working as a high fashion model. Bennie had found us a sublet, in the same building James Dean lived in before he became famous. The apartment was furnished, so we just had to bring our things. Bennie and I immediately became friends. I made rounds all winter and landed a few small roles in some of the nighttime TV dramas then taping in New York: *Studio One, Armstrong Circle Theatre, East Side West Side*, and *The Nurses*. I even landed a commercial for Armstrong Floor Wax, which paid a flat fee for the first thirteen weeks, then started paying residuals when it was picked up for another cycle. I prayed for these residuals to continue as they made it possible to pay the rent without needing to accept a substitute teaching job that week.

As the months went on my mother was adjusting a little bit better to my act of desertion but would not tell any relatives I had moved away from home. She said she didn't want them to think badly of me. Whenever a relative came for a visit I had to come home and pretend I still lived there.

I spent my days making rounds, taking modern jazz dancing with Matt Mattox, and scene study classes with various acting teachers and directors. I continued getting extra work in most of the films that came to shoot in New York and some small parts on the soaps, especially *As The World Turns* and *The Guiding Light*. I was also doing some small theatre projects where, because I looked so young even though I was in my mid-twenties, I was often cast as a teenager. I also did some modeling, although mine was for the various romance magazines with names like *True Romance, True Experience, True Secrets*, and *True*

Love. Actors were used in these shoots, as we had to portray emotional states to illustrate the stories. I posed for various versions of a distraught girl discovering her boyfriend with another date, a rebellious teen shrinking from her parents' shouts and recriminations, to a happy young married being carried over the threshold of her new apartment.

five

Childhood is the kingdom where nobody dies

Edna St. Vincent Millay

1974

As the months dragged on, it became harder to get up each morning and go back to that place of death where my child was waiting for me. By the time I usually got on the cross-town bus, it was almost empty. The school kids and working people had already taken an earlier bus, and I sat in relative isolation, lost in thoughts of what lay ahead. The hardest step was getting off the bus into the bright morning sun and walking into that dark cold hospital lobby.

I knew I had to take Julie out of there. I just needed more time to make myself strong enough to swallow the fear of the future. Each day, I saw her eyes follow me and respond to my words and to the music tapes that she remembered. I watched her cry when she heard the Little Prince sing his song of goodbye to the pilot, and giggle when Peter Pan taught Wendy and her brothers to fly. She talked to me through her eyes and her sounds. I could never, ever, send her to a nursing home.

As time passed I noticed several of the other mothers' bellies growing round. Clearly, the healthy response to having a child on a cancer ward was to become pregnant with another child. I wondered whether if Stu and I had not been divorced, I would have made the same choice.

Each day I walked around the unit and talked to the kids. Some of them I'd met as outpatients when they came in for their chemo regimes and now were further into their battle. Others, I got to know for the first time. I anointed myself "substitute mother," because I was there most of the day. I was there to hold a hand during a shot or stroke a forehead or sing a favorite song to ease a pain. Even teenagers took my hand, while they closed their eyes and perhaps pretended it was their mother's.

When Julie's roommate, a ten year old girl named Elizabeth, started to go into respiratory failure, I held her hand while the staff tried to contact her parents in New Jersey to come before she went into a coma. Julie sensed the tension and cried her ahhs in tandem with my soothing words to Elizabeth. Elizabeth kept calling over to Julie, telling her everything was going to be fine and encouraging me to go over and give Julie a hug also. Finally, I rolled Julie's bed closer to hers so I could sit between them and hold both their hands. I heard myself singing our nighttime songs over and over until Elizabeth's parents arrived. Then I kissed Julie goodnight and went home and cried myself to sleep. The next morning Elizabeth's bed was empty.

There was a small room near the elevators that parents could use as a quiet room or a chapel. I thought a better use of that space would be a padded room, where we could scream our lungs out. I even imagined teaching the song-and-dance exercise, but guessed each parent had probably already found their own screaming space. One mother told me she couldn't wait to get into her car each evening and reach the Long Island Expressway, where she'd close the windows and scream at the top of her lungs. I was sitting in the quiet room one day, waiting for Julie to come back from a test, when I heard a mother talking to another justifying her belief in God. I closed my eyes and gritted my teeth as she proclaimed, "we are the chosen ones because He would not have allowed our children to be inflicted unless He knew we were strong enough to endure this." But I knew there was no God on the children's ward of Memorial Sloan-Kettering.

Each evening, I took the elevator down from the children's floor with its rainbow colored hallways and bright lights that tried to mask the sadness permeating the unit. But the faces of the constantly burned-out staff and the helpless look in parents' eyes behind their forced smiles belied all the rainbow colors that could ever be painted on those walls.

When I got to the lobby, I quickly walked past the sad faces of visitors and outpatients sitting there. As I closed the lobby door behind me and walked toward the bus stop on the corner, it was as if I had been given a temporary reprieve. Most days the sunlight was just starting to wane and I'd feel the warmth of those last rays on my body. As I waited for the cross-town bus to turn into Sixty-Seventh Street and come down the block, I'd breathe in the fresh air, hoping that this would help me wake up from my nightmare. When the bus arrived and opened its door I felt like I was stepping into another world. As we made our way across town the bus began to fill up. I watched the people from this other world as if they were actors in a movie. Some got on laughing and smiling and discussing silly things that happened that day. Some, looking weary from a long day's work, began to relax and make plans for the evening or upcoming weekend. Usually some school kids boarded with their backpacks, on their way home, joking and playfully hitting each other. I looked at the faces before me each day and envied them – no, I was filled with jealousy at their freedom, at their ability to experience happiness. I would have given anything to be like them. I begged the God that I didn't believe in to rewind time and let me wake up before this happened. But instead I was just an observer in this alien world for a few hours each day.

The first thing I did when I got home was take a shower to wash away the stench of death that I felt clinging to my body, then find something to eat in the fridge before crawling into bed with the TV on to soothe me into sleep. Some nights, I would have meaningless sex with Ted, an acquaintance of Stu and mine, who lived in our building. Even though he was married, he had begun to flirt with me after he heard we were divorced. I usually just laughed at his advances, but since Julie was back in the hospital, I accepted the surreal nature of his late night visits—him slipping out of bed while his wife slept and descending the three flights to my apartment. We never talked of his wife, whom I was glad I didn't know, nor did we talk about Julie.

The next day I'd get up and go back to the hospital. There was a bus driver who would stop by during the day in his blue uniform. He was tall and heavyset. His face was weathered; his eyes often glazed with unshed tears and his belly hung a little over his large buckled Transit Authority belt. We would sometimes hang out in the hallway or sit and sip coffee in the lounge and talk about what was on TV the night before. I remember watching his large brown hands holding a paper coffee cup and longing to reach over to touch him and give him a hug. His daughter was in the room next to Julie's. She was in the terminal phase of bone cancer. Then one morning her room was empty, and I missed seeing him.

Children kept dying. I was keeping a list of their names so I wouldn't forget them. Sometimes I wished that Julie would die. But Julie did not die. She didn't get better and she didn't die. Finally, after almost a year, I knew what the right next step was, and I was ready to make it happen.

six

Somewhere I have never traveled, gladly beyond
any experience

e.e.cummings

I said our goodbyes to all the kids and their parents the night before we left for Rusk Rehabilitation Institute and also said a silent goodbye to the almost fifty children who had died during our stay. The next morning, I could hardly wait for the ambulance to come for Julie. When we got to Rusk, I felt as if we were coming out of a dark, sad tunnel into the sunlight. Julie was wheeled into a large, sunny dormitory with six beds around the perimeter. There were large windows on one side of the room facing the East River. Everything felt cheerful and bright. Some of the children in her room were ambulatory, and they came over to her bed to greet her. Her eyes darted from one to another and she began giggling as they introduced themselves. The little girl in the bed next to Julie's was named Daisy. She was around eight years old and able to get about easily in her wheelchair. She only spoke Spanish but did understand some English.

The first few days were filled with examinations and tests to determine what could be accomplished. Julie was started on a physical therapy program aimed at increasing her range of motion and flexibility, and an occupational therapy program to determine whether a means of communication could be established. She was measured for a wheelchair, and a whole list of equipment was ordered to facilitate caring for her at home. I was brought into each session and I numbly watched how to manage her care once we got home. I don't know why the crucial change to a stomach tube for feeding took several weeks to arrange, but once she was wheeled back into her room looking like her old self without a nose tube taped to her face, I began to believe I could actually care for my daughter at home.

A few weeks after Julie moved to Rusk Institute, I boarded the crosstown bus on Thirty-Fourth Street going toward First Avenue to visit her. I was about to put my coins in the slot when a large brown hand covered it. I looked up, and there was my sad-eyed bus driver friend. I was on his bus a few more times that year Julie was at Rusk. He always nodded hello, then held his hand over the coin slot. We talked about the weather or the traffic and never mentioned our pain. His job was to continue his healing, while I was still figuring out what my job was going to be.

My biggest disappointment was that the occupational therapist could not establish a communication system with Julie. It was clear that she did understand what was said to her, but they could find no way to help her voluntarily blink or move her head or eyes to answer a question or express herself. All I had were her facial expressions and her ahhs and cries.

I usually came at noon each day to practice feeding Julie through her stomach tube and to work with the therapists. All this new stimulation and therapy seemed to wake her up. She definitely was more alert to her surroundings and the people around her. My mother also saw the change in her granddaughter's awareness which I think made her visits easier and enjoyable. She visited a few times a week, and on those days I got some respite and was able to get there later in the day. I could see Julie loved having her Grandma there, holding her hand, telling her a story, or singing to her. She was always bright-eyed and smiling when I arrived to take over.

One day as I walked down the hall toward the big room I heard my mother singing, "Daisy, Daisy, Give me your answer true." She was sitting between Julie and Daisy's beds singing to both of them. Julie was giggling and Daisy was joining in whenever she heard her name. These song sessions became a ritual for my mother during the time at Rusk.

She added "East Side, West Side, all around the town," which I also remembered my Nanna singing to me when I was little. And then as an extra treat for both Julie and Daisy she would do the "This little piggy" routine. After that, whenever Daisy saw either my mother or me she would bring her feet out from under the covers and wiggle her toes in the air until one of us would do the tickling part.. Of course, Julie got her toes tickled each time as well.

I thought we would be at Rusk for about a month, but the time kept adding up until I stopped counting the days and weeks. One day the social worker on the unit asked me to drop by her office

"Mrs. Goodman your health insurance is almost depleted. What are your plans?"

"You're the social worker. Aren't you supposed to help me figure that out?"

"Well, I guess I could give you the address of the Medicaid office for you to file a claim."

"Medicaid? You know we're not eligible for Medicaid."

As I stood up and turned to walk out of her office, I added with all the indignation I could muster, "Our insurance is being eaten up because it's taking forever to get us out of this place. Don't you think it's the social worker's job to find a solution for this kind of situation?"

And guess what? She found just the funding program we needed: a Children's Catastrophic Health Care Coverage. When Stu's health insurance went dry, this new plan covered the rest of Julie's hospital stay and in addition helped me finance her health aides when we went home.

It took six months to get Julie home. Those six months at Rusk, not only prepared me to care for Julie at home, but in addition, my life's course was forever changed. When I look back over my relationships it's clear I was always attracted to men. After the teenage crushes, there was Miles, my first true love. Then there was the list of faces with unremembered names that it felt "cool" and grown-up to accumulate, like that James Dean look-alike in summer stock one year, and the tall blond muscular one the next summer.

When I was twenty-five, I met Stu and knew he was my destined true love, although along the way I had had fleeting unacted-upon crushes on women. The first was my high school homeroom teacher, then an actress I met in summer stock, and then an actress I was in an Off Broadway show with and wound up sharing a narrow bed with after a late night rehearsal. I remember my surprise at the sexual stirrings I felt as I lay close to her, unable to fall asleep. Because of these occasional sexual feelings toward women, I thought that perhaps we all had the possibility of falling in love with either a man or a woman.

After Stu and I divorced, my ideal of eternal true love was shattered. I met other men, thought about dating some, but found I had no real interest in any and was even physically turned off by a few—too self centered, too misogynistic, too hairy a body, too boring. Then, while Julie was in Sloan-Kettering I allowed myself to find comfort in Ted's arms.

When we moved to Rusk, I met a young woman named Kim, who was the recreation therapist working with the kids on Julie's floor. She was twenty-three years old, very pretty, with shoulder length light brown hair and an athletic body. We started talking, and each day I found myself looking forward to our meetings. I felt like a mentor to her. She lived on Long Island with her parents while doing this internship at Rusk as part of her Masters program. Kim was fascinated by anything that happened in Manhattan and readily accepted my invitation to join me one evening to hear a friend of mine sing in a cabaret. We went to dinner and then joined two other friends of mine, a lesbian couple, at the cabaret. We drank some wine and listened to my friend sing, as I watched Kim become captivated by my two friends.

Afterwards Kim came back to my apartment rather than make the long trip home to Long Island. I set her up with bed linen and a pillow for the pullout sofa in the living room, said good night, and made my way back to my bedroom to sleep till it was time to go back to Rusk. A few minutes later, Kim came into my bedroom and slipped into bed next to me. There was no need to speak and certainly not to think or analyze.

Kim and I inhabited a magical world for almost a month. At the hospital, she was my daughter's recreation therapist and I the visiting Mom. A few nights a week she stayed in the city, came home with me and shared my bed. By the time I took Julie home from Rusk, Kim's internship had ended and maybe also her sexual experimentation. She went back to her parent's house on Long Island, to school, and probably to her boyfriend, and I never heard from her again.

But my life was forever changed. It was a clear and undeniable fact: I no longer had any interest in a heterosexual relationship. I moved happily forward in my new identity as a lesbian.

seven

Love is a deeper season than reason

e.e.cumming

BACK TO 1964

I met Stu on a Dandee Bread commercial, which was the name Wonder Bread used in its southern markets. I played a young housewife raving about how I loved Dandee Bread and he was the bag boy at the counter packing my purchases. We filmed at a supermarket on the Upper West Side. Stu and I rehearsed our bit with the director and did a walk-through for the camera before our lunch break. We went to lunch together at a little diner near the shoot and I felt attracted to this handsome young actor who looked like a combination Bruce Dern and Robert Goulet, only shorter. He was a recent arrival to New York from a regional theatre company in Montreal, where he had been living.

We dated for about a year, and although our physical attraction was very strong I felt him always distancing himself from me emotionally. I tried to talk with him about the disconnect I was experiencing, but he just laughed it off. Finally I broke off with him and made myself focus on my quest for acting work. Sometimes, late at night, I'd think about Miles, whom I had broken up with a few years before, and wonder whether I'd ever meet someone else I would feel that much in love with– or had I blown my one chance.

The New York theatre scene was like a small town and I continued to run into Stu over the next year at various auditions. We even worked together a few days as extras in the Village, shooting a film with Peter Sellers. As we spent time on the set, I was aware of how much he had opened up emotionally during our year apart and I started to think about him being in my life again.

As we grew closer he told me that when we had first begun dating, he was still recovering from a very painful separation and divorce, which was the reason he left Canada. He had been afraid to open up to the possibility of feeling pain again. But during that year apart, he missed the connection he felt with me and realized he had to take a chance. We began spending more and more time together, either at his apartment or at mine. And, just as in the movies, we began to fall in love.

His lease was about to expire and I was ready to leave my roommate-strewn past behind. We began to look for an apartment together on the Upper West Side. My mother was becoming suspicious of our living arrangement, and I realized the jig was up when I went to her bank to cash a check against her account, as I did from time to time. I felt like a criminal when the clerk said "Sorry I can't cash this check. Your name has been removed from the account." I imagined this as the middle-class equivalent of being disowned. When I called my mother, she ran true to form, ranting about being disgraced and deceived by us after checking the resident hotel I told her Stu was living in. I tried in vain to understand the disgrace she felt when she discovered her twenty-seven-year-old daughter was living with the man she loved.

Stu and I found a wonderful one-bedroom apartment, for $150 a month on the third floor of a converted brownstone on West Sixty-Ninth Street near Central Park. It was the front apartment and our bay window looked out onto the quiet tree-lined street.

As my twenty-eighth birthday loomed, I began to worry about getting too old to have a child. We had only been living together for a year, and I was absolutely committed to making a career in acting, which meant I needed to continue to study, perform in workshops, and be available to take an acting job anywhere. In addition, I didn't think I was emotionally ready to be a mother yet. Then I'd imagine the proverbial clock ticking toward my thirtieth birthday, after which it was considered dangerous to become pregnant. As scary as it seemed one moment, in the next, the idea of becoming a mother felt very romantic and exactly the right thing to do. Stu told me he believed that if we were going to become parents we needed to be officially married. I never felt that a marriage license would make our relationship any more real or solid, but I succumbed to his moral need and we planned to marry.

This decision brought my mother back into the picture, after we had not spoken for more than a year. She organized an engagement party at her house. Aside from our friends, Stu's relatives came in from Philadelphia and met the few cousins I had from my mother's side and her small circle of friends. Happy as my mother was that I would at last become an honest woman, she was upset that Stu's family lived in Philadelphia; her dream of having a new family nearby would not be realized.

I never had an image of myself walking down the aisle in a wedding dress, so we planned an intimate wedding in a chapel at the Stephen Wise Synagogue. Attending our small ceremony were Stu's father and grandmother, who had raised him, and my sister and mother, along with Stu's best friend and his wife. Afterward, we had two weekend receptions in our small apartment, one Sunday with his relatives and friends from Philly, the next for my side. My mother made every effort to cover up the fact that we had already been living in our "new" apartment before the wedding. At one point I saw her closing cabinet doors in people's faces so as not to expose pots and pans that looked used.

Nothing changed for me after our wedding and the two parties, other than now our relationship was official. We went back to our lives, only now with all our new presents: dishes, silverware, shiny pots, pans, kitchen gadgets, and stack of gift certificates for household items and linens. I kept checking but I didn't feel any difference. I loved Stu exactly the same as before. I knew he was my soul mate and we would never part.

One day I heard about an agent who specialized in casting for voice-overs which paid really good money. He set up an audition for me with a producer who was casting actors to dub foreign films into English. The film I auditioned for and got was called *Julie the Red Head*. I was hired to dub into English the voice of a well known French actress named Pascale Petit.

I sat in a sound booth with the English dialog for my character, watching the film scene by scene. I was cued by the director to speak my lines exactly at the moment my character opened her mouth and to end my lines exactly when her mouth stopped moving. The first day I stumbled a bit and didn't fit the lines precisely, but by the end of the day I got the hang of it. Sometimes I was in the sound booth alone recording my lines and sometimes I was with another actor doing a scene. I enjoyed my two weeks as Julie the Redhead and made a good salary.

Julie the Redhead was a popular film on late night TV for about a year and I loved turning it on and hearing my voice come out of Pascale Petit's mouth, even though I wasn't getting paid for any of those replays, as it was a non-union job with no residuals. I was ready to begin a career in dubbing, but nothing else ever materialized. I continued making rounds and sometimes landing a day's work as an extra. As the Sixties drew to a close, this was getting more difficult because more and more evening TV shows were making the move to the West Coast. I was thankful, the soaps and commercials were still shooting in New York and films were still coming here to shoot their exteriors. But mainly, I was just getting extra work on the various soaps: *The Guiding Light, Another World, One Life To Live.*

After my twenty-nineth birthday, I took a deep breath and stopped taking the pill.

One night at a Chinese restaurant a few months later, I had to run to the bathroom, where I threw up my entire dinner. When it happened again at our local Italian restaurant, a few nights later, I thought I had the flu and asked my doctor for an antibiotic. But, after he examined me, he announced, to my joy and my terror, "Congratulations. You're pregnant." This news segwayed into me throwing up and munching saltines for much of the next three months. But then thank goodness, I entered a middle period of great energy and at times positive feelings about my new role in life.

With the new responsibilities he felt about starting a family, Stu began to think about a more secure living than acting. Before coming to New York from Montreal, he had worked regularly as an actor on Canadian TV. During that period he became interested in the camera and spent much of his time observing the cameramen and their technique. Now he began to pour over technical books on TV circuitry from the library. He taught himself how to operate a camera, then bluffed his way into a job as a cameraman for ABC-TV. In the beginning, each day before he went to work, I'd beg him not to electrocute himself.

By this time I was six months pregnant and could no longer hide my belly under the then-fashionable A-line dresses. I reluctantly stopped making rounds and very happily said no to all calls for substitute teaching.

It was a new experience for us having a regular salary coming in each week, plus as a full time employee Stu was entitled to two weeks vacation with pay. This was a first in either of our lives: "a paid vacation." When he came home with this amazing news, we decided to treat ourselves to the honeymoon we never took. We both loved warm weather and beaches, and we began looking for a Caribbean island on which to celebrate our new life together. We arranged to go in November, before rates went up for the holidays. Nelson Rockefeller had just won his third term as Governor, with John Lindsey being elected mayor, defeating Abraham Beame and William Buckley.

The resort we chose was Little Dix Bay, part of the British West Indies. It was in a remote part of the island and offered separate little cottages on stilts right on the beach front. Their ads promised crystal clear waters teaming with brightly colored fish and coral reefs a hundred feet below our catamaran, as we snorkeled nearby. We were sold and booked our flights immediately. I had not been on a plane since I was eleven years old, when my parents had me accompany my grandmother to Texas for an operation. Now seventeen years later, I was flying with my husband on a super jet to the Bahamas, then boarding a tiny eight-seater twin engine plane and holding my breath and his hand tightly, as we flew low over bright blue water, and landed on a short dirt runway fifteen minutes later. This was much more exciting than my wedding day.

We were treated like royalty by the staff. Our little cottage on the beach was like living in a fantasy. To make it even more surreal, we spent an afternoon on a catamaran with Governor Rockefeller's two brothers, who were there vacationing after his election. We awoke each morning to the sun shining through the shutters, put on our bathing suits, and walked along the sand to the open-air dining room. After breakfast we went shelling along the beach or donned our snorkel masks and fins and practiced our newly learned skills in those clear-as-crystal blue waters, just as the ads had promised. I had never been a good swimmer, but once I put on the snorkel mask and fins and kicked off I felt like an Olympian and lost myself exploring the world below. On this vacation, we both fell in love with the brightly colored tropical shells that we later began to make into jewelry.

After our ten days in paradise we flew home, tanned and rested. We put our beautiful new shells on display on a shelf in our bookcase, developed our pictures, and gradually got back to real life. Stu continued working at ABC, while I now had a lot of free time. One day I was sitting on the couch looking at all magnificent shapes and colors of the shells we had brought home and began to think of ways to use them creatively. Maybe we could put some of them together in a collage. Maybe we could figure out how to mount them and use them in pieces of jewelry. As my tummy was growing, my mind was musing over this new idea.

eight

My belly continued to grow, and when I felt my baby move about and saw its little feet kicking out, I felt a thrill, even though there was a nagging fear deep inside–I couldn't yet see myself as a mother. Julie Harris was my acting idol, and when I read that she had her child by natural childbirth, I was determined to do the same. This was a new phenomenon in the mid-sixties and not all doctors or hospitals were yet open to the concept of giving the expectant mother control of her delivery.

I found Dr. Buchman who agreed to natural childbirth–and he had admitting privileges at New York Hospital, which was the only hospital in the city allowing the husband into the delivery room. He referred us to Elizabeth Bing, the pioneer in this type of delivery, and we joined her Lamaze classes. Along with five other couples, we attended weekly classes in the special breathing techniques and teamwork approach that we would need to deliver our children. Stu and I practiced these techniques at home; me doing the special breathing and puffing, with Stu happily taking on the role of directing and cheering me on. In those days there were no sonograms, only old wives tales. My landlady told me I would have a girl because I was carrying so high and forward. She didn't mention the hiatal hernia and indigestion this position also created in my last two months. I wanted a girl so badly, as I couldn't envision myself as the mother of a boy. Julie would be her name, of course.

As a just-in-case backup, if I had a boy, I chose Kim, from John Steinbeck's *The Red Pony*.

The crib and dressing table from Best & Co., along with an enormous gift basket of everything anyone would ever need for a new baby arrived, the week before my due date; compliments of my mother. When I went for my weekly exam the next day, Dr. Buchman asked me if all was ready at home. He was right, because two mornings later, at 5:00 am, I woke up thinking I wet the bed. When it dawned on me my water broke, I woke Stu to call Dr. Buchman and get us ready to go to the hospital. As I started to get dressed, my contractions began. By the time Stu packed my lollipops, to keep my mouth moist as I puffed, and his snacks, to keep him going while he coached, my contractions were only ten minutes apart. I felt as if I were in a dream as we walked down the two flights of stairs from our apartment into the dawn and hailed a cab to take us through Central Park to New York Hospital. We checked in, and I was wheeled to a prep room and then into another room to continue my breathing and puffing regime. Stu joined me, along with a wonderful nurse who knew exactly where and how to rub my lower back as the "contractions" deepened into extreme pain. We were brainwashed in our Lamaze classes with the word "contraction." At no time was the word pain ever used. But what I was experiencing was clearly pain, not contraction. Stu kept rubbing my back the way that nurse showed him as my contractions became closer and closer. A resident kept popping in to measure my dilation.

Dr. Buchman appeared suddenly, reassuring me all was going well as he quickly whisked me into the delivery room. Aside from the unbelievable pain I was feeling, the atmosphere in that little delivery room was bustling with positive energy. I had a team of cheering nurses, with Stu at my side counting out my breathing and puffing combinations and Dr. Buchman directing the show. Very soon I was told I could push, and push I did. Then, accompanied by loud cheers, Stu and I saw a head appear in the mirror above me. After one final push, I heard the magical words: "You got your Julie." Julie was born at 10:30 a.m. March 4th, 1967, five hours after I arrived at the hospital.

Stu went to call my mother and sister and his father and grandmother. I was wheeled to a room with three other mothers, with our babies in an adjoining nursery. We attended sessions with a nurse, who guided us in how to hold our babies, change them and feed them. At first none of this felt real to me as

I watched myself moving about the nursery in my new role as a mother. But by the second day, as I continued to care for this little being, I started to feel a deep connection to the miracle I was holding in my arms.

Julie was a beautiful baby— no wrinkles, no reddened skin, just a six-pound, seven-ounce, perfect, smiling, alert being. The only problem was every time I fed her a bottle—I had no desire to breast feed— and returned her to her crib, she would cry loudly and unceasingly until she turned blue. No matter how many times the nurses assured me that she was fine, I couldn't stop worrying. I asked to speak with Dr. Buchman, but instead a resident appeared. Without even a look in the direction of my blue-faced crying daughter, he started to question me about my "overconcerns" on becoming a mother. I held back the immense anger rising inside me toward this unfeeling robot lecturing me, and, in as calm a voice as I could get out between my clenched teeth, thanked him for his advice. As soon as he left, I went to a phone booth on the floor and called Dr. Buchman. He said he would ask a pediatrician to come to the hospital to examine her.

The next morning that pediatrician's partner came in his place to examine Julie, as he was at a conference. The partner seemed warm and friendly and best of all recognized that Julie was having a problem not me. He assured me she was a healthy baby. He thought she could be having a problem digesting the current formula and suggested a change, and also that I make an appointment with him after we got home to assess her digestion further.

The shells and our plans for making jewelry were put on the back burner for the next few months as my new role of mother occupied me day and night. Once in while I'd catch myself feeling as if I were an observer watching myself performing my motherly chores—as though I was in a play. But more often, when I held her in my arms, I felt such incredible love and connection to my exquisite baby that I'd fill with tears. Stu was a wonderful help and seemed to enjoy his new role as father. When he was home, he was always available to change a diaper or do a middle-of-the-night feeding. At one point, ABC asked him to do the camera work on the Gemini space launch. I was alone with Julie for a week, and we both managed to survive. I looked forward to Stu's nightly calls, and we kept a count of all the overtime pay he was earning for this assignment, knowing that this was bringing us closer to being able to move to a larger apartment.

Julie's digestive problems continued even with the new formula. I made an appointment with the pediatrician we saw in the hospital, and he now suggested I try her on soy milk formula, which did the trick. She was able to digest it better and her crying stopped. This made an enormous difference in our lives, as we could actually relax and enjoy a whole meal without her crying.

Once we had made this contact with the partner doctor, I never changed back to the original recommended one. I've always wondered whether if I had, would Julie's life been saved.

nine

but love is the sky and I am for you
just so long and long enough

e.e.cummings

It was a thrill for me when Julie began talking and putting words together at around five or six months, and my connection with her grew stronger as we began having conversations. She stayed bald till she was almost two, then began to grow light brown hair with some blonde highlights. My sister and I both had red hair as children, with mine gradually turning to light brown, but my sister remained a redhead. Julie's eyes stayed bright blue; in spite of Stu's dark hair and brown eyes, the Ellenbogen genes came through.

In February 1968, when Julie was about ten months old, Stu was plucked from the evening news crew to go to Grenoble, France. His assignment was to cover the ski events at the Winter Olympics. He and his camera were stationed at a point three-fourths of the way to the top of the mountain, to track the skiers as they made their way down the major slope. It was his camera that captured Jean-Claude Killy as he sped down to win his three gold medals in alpine skiing that year. Whenever Stu called, his excitement was contagious, making me feel I was there with him as he proudly recounted his day.

When he got back from France, we began looking for a larger apartment. I always was enthralled with a large building on West End Avenue and Seventy-Fourth Street. A friend of mine from Performing Arts had lived there with her parents, and I had fallen in love with the idea of living in a doorman and elevator-manned building. We had no idea how expensive it would be, but we took

35

a chance and asked the doorman whether there were any apartments available. We were shown an apartment with one very large bedroom, a bathroom next to it, and a smaller bedroom that was the perfect size for Julie. The rent was $250 a month, $100 more than we were presently paying. We took a deep breath and signed the lease. A few weeks later, right after Julie's first birthday, we said goodbye to our friends in the brownstone and moved into our new apartment.

Around the same time, Stu was asked to do camera on a new soap. It was called *Dark Shadows* and it progressed over the next year from being just a soap to a cult classic. Its vampire plot and elaborate special effects fed into Stu's creativity, and his camera work and knack in tracking dramatic action was noticed and appreciated. I watched with pride as he came into his own as a craftsman.

Stu's involvement with this show was also a great break for me as an actress. He introduced me to the casting director, who began to call me in whenever they needed a young girl extra. One day, I was asked to play the waitress at the restaurant where the characters often met. From then on whenever they did a scene at The Blue Whale Restaurant, I was called in. I usually didn't have any lines, but once in a while I was asked to say "good evening" or "here's your order," which upgraded me to a speaking background actor and an additional salary.

My career took another move forward when Burt Brinkerhoff, with whom I had been in an acting class, called to tell me he was directing a new play called *Saturday Night*. It was to star his wife, Zina Jasper and he wanted to know if I'd like to be her understudy. I jumped at the chance to be in a real production rather than the showcases I had done up till then. It was going to be produced at The Sheridan Square Playhouse, on the corner of Seventh Ave and Eighth Street in the Village, a prestigious Off-Broadway theatre at that time, with a listing in the theatre section of all the newspapers.

Being as understudy is a frustrating job, with a glimmer of hope of doing the role at some point if there is a long run. When the play went into previews, I sat in the audience, watching each night and internally noting all Zina's moves and lines. When the play opened, I came to the theatre each evening at half hour and could stay or leave once the curtain rose on Act One. The play got good reviews for Zina and the other actors and for the playwright, Jerome Kass, who was predicted to be a new force in the theatre, and who later married Nora Ephron's sister, Delia. As the run continued, I was able to stay home on alert, which meant dressed with hair in rollers ready to hop a cab down to the Village if Zina was unable to go on. I got comfortable staying home with Julie, and some nights even prayed not to get a call. I never felt completely rehearsed enough and worried about whether I would be able to carry it off if I ever got that call. Whenever I read about an understudy going on at the last minute and bringing down the house, I wondered how I would have done.

After the show closed, I fell back into my routine of taking class and making rounds. In November, when Julie was two and a half, Stu and I planned for our annual vacation. We picked Club Med, which had all inclusive packages in some of the great snorkeling and diving areas in the Caribbean, and booked a two-week stay in their Guadeloupe village in the French West Indies. My mother, whom I don't remember ever hugging me or my sister, had transformed into an extremely loving and hugging grandmother. She even agreed to take care of Julie for the two weeks Stu and I would be away. The night before our flight, we brought Julie to my mother in diapers. Miraculously when we came back two weeks later, she was in underpants. My mother shrugged and said, "I just took off her diapers and asked her to tell me when she needed to go."

Stu went back to *Dark Shadows* but was soon tapped as the onstage camera-man for the Dick Cavett Show, which was shot live and had a much less stress-ful schedule. Now that I was home with Julie, I began to work more and more with the shells we had collected. Stu had some design ideas, and we began to search for chains and findings in the various novelty stores in the West Thirties. Stu's dentist gave him some old drills, and we began to experiment with drilling holes in some of our shells as well. For some designs we used leather and mac-ramé cords. We mounted the designs we liked best on velvet boards and took them around to the many clothing and accessory stores on the Upper West Side. Several stores asked us to leave pieces on consignment. When we checked back a few weeks later, they had sold and we were asked for more. As we got more orders we realized we needed help in putting our designs together. I hired some unemployed actor friends and taught them how to use a pinch-nosed pli-ers, epoxy, and chain cutters. Soon, several afternoons a week, there were three or four actors sitting around a bridge table in our living room putting orders together for shipment.

Somehow, we had created a business. Our selling point was that each piece was handmade and featured designs using unique shells in their natural state.

Stu was a born salesman and sold several dozen pieces to Bloomingdales and Bendel, as well as Lord and Taylor, and then got orders for new designs when they sold. That summer, my sister, who was now a lawyer, was part of a group house rental in the Hamptons. She offered us the house whenever it was not in use. Stu and I and Julie spent our mornings selling our jewelry to the shops in Southampton, East Hampton, Amagansett and Montauk. In the afternoons, we went to the beach.

After a year with the Dick Cavett Show, Stu was asked to go on the road for ABC Sports. He became their handheld cameraman during the football season, and also for the NASCAR events. For most of the next year and a half, I'd help Stu pack his bags on a Thursday and not see him till the following Monday. Once he began going on the road, I felt our relationship changing. He was more distant when he was home, and I was feeling neglected. Then we began to fight. One night, while packing his bags for his next trip, I found a condom in one of the side pockets. For the first time, the idea that he might be having an affair crossed my mind. I was too afraid of hearing the answer to confront him, so I kept my mouth shut and tried to swallow my growing anger as our fighting continued to escalate.

I kept busy with the shell orders and taking care of Julie. At Christmastime, Julie and I traveled with him to Florida for the North-South game. Afterward, we had a week in the sun together as a family, which seemed to help our relationship. But by the time Julie and I joined him in Miami for the second Christmas, we had trouble saying two words to each other without a fight. I dreaded the emptiness I felt whenever we left other people and came back to the hotel room at night. Julie was almost five. Stu and I had been together for seven years, and I had thought our love was so strong we would be together forever. But our life had turned into an ever-repeating nightmare. I didn't know why we were fighting, and I didn't have any idea how to stop it and make things go back to the way they were before. Instead, I forced myself to focus on Julie, the jewelry, and my acting classes.

When we first began collecting shells and making the jewelry, we fantasized about going to Tahiti on one of our yearly vacations. So we began to plan our trip, hoping that the magical island of Tahiti would heal our anger and bring us back together again.

Around this time, we stopped by a local boutique where we had previously sold a few dozen pieces, to show a new design we made with a heart shell especially for Mother's Day. Sitting in the store talking to the owners was Joan Cook, a feature writer for the *New York Times*. She became intrigued with the story of our fledgling business and wrote a piece about us that appeared in the Style section the next week. There was a picture of us and a story about the young couple who had started their own shell jewelry business and were now planning their dream trip to Tahiti.

An editor at Crown Press saw the *Times* article and called to set up a meeting to explore our interest in writing a book about making shell jewelry for their craft book series. He asked us to develop an outline and also write a sample chapter with pictures. I had written a bit in college and Stu certainly could take pictures and we both could explain the step-by-step process in making a piece of jewelry, so we accepted the assignment.

We submitted our work to him, and he called us to come in to sign a contract. We had a year to complete the book and would receive a set fee up front, then royalties as the book sold. He wished us well on our upcoming trip to Tahiti and said he was looking forward to working with us. We kept our mouths shut about our marital difficulties and went home with visions of the $70,000 he said their current macrame book was netting the author, dancing in our heads. But by this time, our relationship had deteriorated to the point that we couldn't even have a conversation without it turning into a fight. It was clear that we would not be able to take our dream trip to Tahiti. Instead we took Woody Allen's advice: *why go on an expensive trip for two weeks when for the same money we could get a divorce which would last forever.* We decided to separate, go to couples therapy, and see what happened. I told Julie that Daddy was going to be on the road for a while, and Stu moved out and into an apartment about a block away.

We still had to write the book, so we divided the chapters between us, with Stu taking the descriptive photos using an actress friend of mine who agreed to do the modeling in return for head shots. We met once a week to go over each other's chapter and plan the needed photos. I acted as calm and detached as I could whenever we met and afterwards cried my eyes out. In the midst of this drama, we kept going to our couples counselor, together and individually. After a few months of these sessions, I still felt as alienated from Stu as I did before. When I finally had enough courage to admit this to our therapist in my individual session, he shocked me by saying "Perhaps it was time for me to let go of the idea that our marriage could be repaired."

I called Stu's apartment one day to relay our editor's request for a progress report meeting, and a woman's voice answered "Hi, who's this?" I was so flustered that I just hung up without a word. Hearing that young woman's voice, forced me to face what I was pretending would never happen. I finally let myself feel anger toward Stu, anger toward his deceit, his lies, his cowardice in having me hold onto a hope that was gone. Once I did, I felt free to truly grieve and then move on. I was able to stop lying to Julie that Daddy would be coming home soon and she would be able to climb into bed with us both again. I assured her that he would still see and spend time with her, but she had a hard time understanding and accepting that Daddy was not going to be living with us any longer. That voice on the other end of the phone eventually became the first of his next two brief marriages to young women in their early twenties. Through all my upset and anger and sadness, we finished the book and submitted it to our editor, and I got up the nerve to call my sister and tell her I was ready to file for divorce.

A few months later, our editor called with the news that our book had just come off the presses and the publicity department was setting up department-store and daytime TV talk-show appearances for us. Even then, we decided not to tell our editor about our separation as we were fearful it would affect their publicity planning.

I had been so relieved not to have to see Stu after we finished the writing; I couldn't bear the thought of now having to be with him again. I suggested that he handle the magazine articles and interviews about diving and collecting shells, which were his interests, and I do the bulk of the personal appearances. We did a joint interview only when it couldn't be avoided, including the ABC TV interview Stu had arranged with Rosanne Scermadella in our supposed home living room.

I was in my most glorious fantasy world, seeing my picture in *New York Times* ads and appearing at Bloomingdale's and Macy's, giving demonstrations on jewelry making and signing books for throngs of shell enthusiasts. In 1972, there were several daytime TV talk shows featuring segments on various topics, including new books as well as actors touting their newest films. During that first whirlwind year of publication, I sat down with Dinah Shore and Joyce Brothers. And one morning I was driven to NBC-TV by limousine to appear on a morning talk show with a new personality named Barbara Walters. She ignored me totally, never even saying hello until we were on camera, while fawning over the next guest who was a home lighting expert. I must say I did feel my inadequacy after that experience.

ten

I have been one acquainted with the night

Robert Frost

With the publication of our book and the publicity it engendered, we began to receive orders for shells and jewelry findings, along with fan letters about the book, including stories from the writers about their love of shells and their experiences around shells. I answered many of the letters and maintained a correspondence with some of our repeat customers.

We also gained an agent for our jewelry line who sold our designs to the Neiman Marcus and the Broadway chains, both of which owned stores all around the country. Not only did this give us more orders than I could produce with my small band of actor friends, but we also needed to continue creating new designs for each selling season. One of our contacts suggested a company in the jewelry district that did piece work at a much faster rate than we were doing around my bridge table. We were now in business for real.

Our editor reported our book was still selling well. We were now in most public libraries in the country and also in most of the craft stores and shell shops. One day he called to tell us we were going into our second printing and a soft cover trade edition was being planned. In spite of this news, our sales were nowhere near Crown's macramé book success, and the publicity department seemed to be losing ideas for additional marketing.

I was on my own with Julie and supporting myself to some extent with the business, with Stu continuing to pay our rent until I got a job. But I still had not given up my dream of an acting career. Now that there was nothing and no one to keep me in New York, I was free to go wherever the work was. I began to imagine relocating to Los Angeles, as TV and film production in New York had all but evaporated. This would be the perfect time to check out LA to see whether I'd have a better chance for acting work if Julie and I moved out there.

I told the publicity people at Crown I was planning a trip to the West Coast on personal business, which I was willing to pay for, and asked them to set up TV and book store events around the LA area. They promised to arrange prime events.

As my wounds began to heal, I tried to make myself open to meeting and dating someone new. Friends introduced me to a few men, but each time, when they opened their mouths, they sounded self- involved and egotistical and no sparks flew for me. I wasn't feeling lonely because Julie was with me. I took her to restaurants and even to a motel in East Hampton for a week, the first summer. Sitting with her in a restaurant and walking with her on the beach, I was able to fend off the few men who tried to flirt with me. Julie was only five and could start school anywhere we lived. Once I decided to make the trip West, I contacted a few acting and directing friends who had already relocated. After the publicity department set up my appearances and ordered our books shipped to their West Coast delivery sources, I made flight reservations for Julie and me and our little grey poodle, Dorie (nee Dorian Grey), who had recently become part of our fractured family. He was allowed on board in a little carry-ing case in which he could sleep under our seats, and we were allowed to hold him on our laps for short periods.

Friends suggested we stay at the Chateau Marmot, which at that time was still an inexpensive charming European style old hotel that attracted a young and not yet famous theatrical crowd along with a few reclusive movie stars. It was situated high on a hill just off Sunset Boulevard, near Schwab's Drug Store, where, legend says, Lana Turner had been discovered sitting at the counter. The highlight of my mornings was breakfast around the pool while a naked Carol Lynley, a young starlet I had seen in films, took her morning swim before retir-ing for the rest of the day to her penthouse apartment. This was several years before the Chateau obtained notoriety when John Belushi was found dead in one of the poolside cottages after an overdose of heroin, and then celebrity status as *the* hotel of Hollywood stars.

I took Julie with me to the morning TV shows which had been booked for me. One was very popular. The host was Tom Snyder, who had not yet been discovered and come east to NBC nighttime TV. He was very kind and interested in our interview and even called Julie over to say hello and ask whether she ever helped Mommy make jewelry. Julie was more interested in looking at the camera and her image in the TV monitor. After the show, the stage manager gave me the phone number of someone who called in saying she was an old friend. It was a casting agent from New York who had hired me a few times and now lived in LA. She happened to be watching the show as she dressed for work. Of course I met with her and added her to the positive side of my "moving or not moving to LA" list. Julie and I also visited with some New York transplanted friends who were now working in TV production.

One day I walked over to Rodeo Drive and sold some of our designs to two very popular clothing stores with the "in" crowd. My pro list was growing by the day and I was seriously thinking of making the big move.

During our last few days in LA, Julie developed a fever and a headache. When we got back to NY she still had the headache and I took her to Dr. Feder, who said he could find nothing wrong and I should just give her Tylenol. Over the next few days the headaches continued, now along with joint pains, especially in her forearms and calves. I took her back to Feder, who now said she may have some sort of virus and put her on an antibiotic.

Our book was still selling, but our publisher's earlier dreams of *Art From Shells* becoming Crown Publishers next craft book sensation seemed to be wavering; our publicity stints were drying up and I figured they had begun to put their efforts into their next project. Our jewelry sales continued to expand and profit from the book's exposure, and I was still reading the trades and making rounds whenever I could.

A week later Julie was still in pain and began to have moments of uncontrolled rage, pulling at my clothing and even tearing the buttons off. One day when visiting Stu, she read a book about colors. When she got home that night she was crying, "Daddy kept yelling at me for saying the wrong color, but my eyes knew the color was blue and not green."

The next day I called Dr. Feder and insisted he see her as soon as possible. He asked me to meet him at New York Hospital, where he was visiting patients. He examined her again and again said, "nothing is wrong." We shared a cab with him when we left and he saw Julie all of a sudden start tearing at my clothes and screaming uncontrollably. He declared she was acting out due to my separation from Stu. I was incensed with his ridiculous diagnosis and insisted that he do further tests. He reluctantly agreed to in-depth testing.

I had been struggling to keep separating my life from Stu whenever possible. But now, with this scary new development, I called him to accompany us to the hospital the next morning for the tests. The resident began his exam by looking into Julie's eyes with a flashlight, then blurted out, "My god, any doctor examining her would see she has a mass in her brain." He immediately arranged a CAT scan. Julie asked us to go with her as a nurse helped her get comfortable on a stretcher. Then, as the valium she had been given began to make her drowsy, she calmly nodded and smiled at me as I explained, "The doctor is going to take you for another exam to try and figure out what is wrong in your head. Don't worry. Daddy and I will be right here waiting for you." We both kissed her and watched as she was wheeled down a long hallway.

Stu and I sat in shock in the waiting room until the resident came out and sat down next to us, saying the CAT scan confirmed there was a tumor pressing against the left side of her brain. He held his hands together in a circle, saying it was about the size of a small saucer and he was immediately admitting her to the hospital.

When Dr. Feder showed up a few hours later as her admitting doctor, I screamed "Don't come near Julie ever again." All I want from you is a referral to the best neurosurgeon in the world and then get the hell out of our lives." He stood there for a few seconds, then turned to the resident, saying he would arrange for some referrals. I met briefly with two neurosurgeons and chose the most positive-sounding one to direct her care. But Feder wouldn't go away. I continued to ignore him as he visited and examined Julie every day during her hospitalization. Afterward, he had the nerve to send a bill for those visits.

I was thirty-five years old, medically naïve, and in no way prepared to deal with life- and- death decisions. I didn't realize it at the time, but Stu was even more naïve than I as we were forced into contact over the fate of our daughter. My mother and sister were just as unprepared and equally unable to face the scenario that was presented to us.

Stu came with me to meet with the surgeon I chose. He was a tall and very officious-looking older man, but with a kind and caring manner. He led us to the chairs opposite his desk and waited till we sat before he spoke.

"Your daughter has a highly malignant brain tumor that can probably be grossly removed by surgery. But the likelihood is it has already metastasized. What we can do is give her radiation afterward to help contain the spread of the cells."

My head started spinning, and I felt as if I was going to faint. Then from a distance I heard his voice say, "One is never sure, but my educated medical guess, given the nature of her tumor, is that she probably will not live more than six months."

As he stood to usher us out of his office, he added that he would also explore any experimental chemotherapy that might help prolong her life. I think I shook his hand and thanked him. I felt Stu guiding me to a bench outside the office. We sat in silence for a few minutes. Then, as I turned to him for advice on what we should do now, he asked me what "metastasized" meant.

eleven

1975

It was the day before Thanksgiving 1975. Julie was eight and a half years old, and after two years in hospitals she was on her way home. Her bright blue eyes were fixed on me as our ambulance weaved in and out of all the holiday traffic. She was lying comfortably, wrapped in a blanket, on a stretcher next to me. I leaned over toward her till our noses touched.

"Julie we're going home. You're going to be sleeping in your own room and Dorie is going to be licking your face."

Her face broke into a wide smile at the mention of Dorie and started giggling and ahhhhh-ahhhing. Sitting there, holding her hand in the ambulance that was transporting us cross-town from Thirty-Fourth Street and First Avenue through the crowded streets and then up Broadway to Seventy-Fourth Street, I was petrified worrying of what lay ahead. Then the siren started to blare.

"We'll never get through this mess otherwise," the driver called back to me as he changed lanes and sped through a red light. I squeezed Julie's hand as she continued her ahhs and giggles. The siren blared on and I could feel my heart beating faster and faster as we got closer to home.

With us in the ambulance was Maggie, the home attendant I had hired. She was a sweet older woman who had been a part-time night nurse on the children's unit at Rusk and wanted to transfer to home care.

When the ambulance driver wheeled Julie into our lobby, John, her favorite doorman who used to stand with her waiting for the school bus each morning, rushed over to say, "Welcome home." Her eyes were taking in everyone as we made our way through the lobby, onto the elevator, and up to our apartment. Dorie started barking and jumping up to greet us as I unlocked the door and

Julie was wheeled at long last into her bedroom, which now resembled a hospital room. Her bed was pushed over to the far wall for Maggie to sleep in, and a large hospital bed with her favorite doll, Elizabeth, and a few of her cuddly stuffed animals by her pillow now dominated the center of the room. A suction machine and other medical paraphernalia took over her night table. I had given away her long worktable and all her art supplies. The dolls that used to live on and under that table in various family groupings were now in a box in her closet.

It felt strange to finally have Julie home again. Our always sunny apartment now felt darker, with an aura of sadness hanging over it. As I adapted to making life easier for us both at home, I soon traded in the monster wheelchair, which was so heavy and cumbersome one needed to be an Olympic weightlifter to use it, for a lightweight stroller with a seating insert that fit her tiny body a hundred times better. Maggie was there to care for Julie, but as the days went on I began to think I had made a mistake in hiring this woman to come home with us. I couldn't put my finger on anything specific, but there was something about her that made me think she was on the verge of falling apart. The first hint was her obsession with counting and recounting the pills that Julie needed to take each day.

Whenever I walked into the kitchen, there she was with all of Julie's pills spread out before her, counting them and recording the sums on an elaborate chart. One evening, when I came in to cook dinner, she was in a panic.

"Oh my God, my God, there is a pill missing. I don't know where it is. I don't know what to do." I'm going to be in trouble." She emptied the bottle again and began to recount.

"Don't worry, Maggie, you won't get into trouble. This isn't the hospital. It's OK." I babbled on trying to soothe her. Finally she seemed to calm down and went back to Julie's room to feed her. But I saw her recounting the pills later that night.

The days passed slowly, with Maggie moving Julie's body in the various range-of- motion exercises every few hours to keep her from becoming atrophied, feeding her through her feeding tube, and attending to all her other basic needs. Days turned into weeks, as I tried to pretend life was back to normal. Each day I made myself leave the apartment for at least a few hours: to have lunch with a friend, to sit in a movie, to check in at the workshop that was now assembling our jewelry orders. I also found myself spending time with one of the women whom I had met with Kim that first night.

Late one night as I was going to bed, Maggie came into my room very agitated. "Mrs. Goodman something is wrong with Julie. She isn't breathing right"

I ran to Julie's room. What I saw was Julie in a deep sleep, her usually clenched arms and hands relaxed, and with a slight smile on her face.

"Everything is fine, Maggie. Don't worry."

"No, she isn't breathing right. There is something wrong," she kept repeating, more agitated each time.

I didn't want this hysterical woman to wake up my sleeping child. So I slid the bed rail down, scooped Julie up into my arms, and carried her to my bed. "Maggie, don't worry. I'll watch over her. Just get some sleep."

A short while later, the phone rang. It was Stu. "Leni, what's going on? Your nurse is hysterical. She said Julie is not breathing and she started begging me to come over now and take her away from you."

"Stu, she's fine. She's sleeping soundly next to me. Maggie's crazy. I'm going to have to get someone else. Hang on. The doorbell's ringing."

When I opened the door, there were two very large policemen standing there. The larger one said, "We received a phone call that your child is dead and that you're hiding her."

I tried to stay grounded in reality as this surreal scene unfolded. My mind was racing, searching for a rational response.

"I don't know what you're talking about. My daughter is sleeping peacefully in my room."

"May we see her?" the same officer asked. I could sense Maggie standing in the background.

"Ah, sure, I guess so." I wondered whether I could deny them access or ask for a warrant, as they did on the TV police shows. But then I thought that might make me look guilty. "She's fast asleep. Could you please tiptoe in so as not to wake her," I heard myself saying in a very authoritative voice.

I led them into my darkened bedroom and over to the bed. I realized Stu was still on the phone. "Stu can you believe she called the police? I'll call you back."

They both bent over my bed and one of them shined a flashlight onto Julie's sleeping, smiling face. After about ten seconds of watching her breathe, they seemed satisfied and quietly walked out of the bedroom toward the living room, where the larger one called in a false alarm on his two-way radio. Maggie was still hovering in the hallway as they walked toward the door.

I stopped them from leaving. "I don't feel safe having this woman here. Please do me a favor and escort her out of my apartment."

They nodded and directed Maggie to get her things together and stood in the hallway till she was ready. Then they said goodnight and escorted her to the elevator. She never said a word to me, nor I to her.

I called Stu back to fill him in. He stayed on the phone as I spewed out my anger about that crazy woman and then slowly calmed down and let it go. As I held the phone to my ear and heard his voice, caring, but now distant and separated from Julie and me, it became crystal clear that I was truly on my own. After I hung up, I sat on the edge of the bed for a few minutes. I smiled as I imagined him going back to bed next to his twenty-something new wife and telling her what had happened and how he handled everything. Then, exhausted, I crawled under the covers next to Julie and closed my eyes to sleep. Aside from the fact that I was now without a caretaker for Julie, I was relieved Maggie was gone and amazed at how well I'd taken care of the situation. I couldn't wait till morning to tell everyone I knew about this absurd night.

The phone woke me at seven. Julie had rolled over a bit but was still fast asleep. "Mrs. Goodman, this is Andy, the doorman. There's been a lady sitting here in the lobby all night. She says she's Julie's nurse and can't leave her post."

"Thank you, Andy. Don't worry, I'll get rid of her."

I called the agency, told the woman what happened, gave her the lobby phone number, and asked for a replacement nurse. She apologized and said she would send someone as soon as possible. I was sure they'd realize Maggie was crazy, but I found out later they believed the stories she told them about my "bizarre" behavior. The next nurse the agency sent confided in me after several months that the agency continued to call her weekly, to see whether I had locked her in the back room yet when I had company, or forbidden her to use any of my plates.

"Why did you take this assignment if you thought I was crazy?"

"Oh, I've been in situations like that and worse. One woman got hysterical when I hung my coat in her closet."

Try as I might to act impeccably hospitable, I felt she and the agency people were waiting for me to slip one day and show my true colors. I just prayed they'd send Maggie on another job where she would lose it again, so they'd finally believe me.

Several more nursing aides followed, and as I gained confidence in myself and my decision to bring Julie home, I also got smarter in choosing the right person and smarter in working the health care system. Instead of using the constant revolving door of health aides the agency sent, I convinced the agency people of the extent of Julie's disabilities and talked them into letting me find a more qualified caretaker on my own who then would join the agency.

After a few more months of dreary days for Julie in a hospital bed in a darkened room, or sitting with a nurse in her stroller in front of the TV, I was ready to explore a new and controversial physical therapy program called patterning.

twelve

Two roads diverged in a wood, and I-
I took the one less traveled by,
And that has made all the difference.

Robert Frost

A friend had sent me an article about patterning when Julie was still at Sloan-Kettering. I filed it in the back of my mind when I made plans to move her to Rusk Institute to see first what traditional rehab could accomplish. There I watched as the physical therapists stretched and moved her and fruitlessly tried to elicit any voluntary movement. I watched as the occupational therapists searched in vain for a way for her to communicate. Then I was handed the instruction sheet for her range-of-motion exercises and told it was time to take her home–with a feeding tube still taped to her stomach and no hope for anything more.

Just before we left Rusk I made an appointment with Dr. Greenspan, the head doctor, who months before had so kindly agreed to take Julie in as a patient, to say thank you and goodbye and arrange for outpatient follow-up. I asked what he thought about patterning. At the mention of that word, he lost the fatherly demeanor he usually exhibited and angrily stated, "I will not continue to see Julie if you go down that road. It is an abusive technique, and I and the American Board of Pediatricians have strong objections to it."

I sat there with my mouth open. "Ah, ah, well what road do you suggest? Why shouldn't I try anything that might help stimulate her?"

By this time he was standing at his desk in full lecture mode. "I am telling you that it is a destructive program. Number one, it is such an extremely demanding commitment that it drives families apart."

That's no problem for me, I thought. My family is already apart.

"Number two, moving a child against their will is child abuse."

I was thinking that Julie would probably love the feeling of moving, but I decided not to argue. I needed him to recommend the twenty-four- hour homecare people from what was left of Stu's health insurance and the additional emergency funding the social worker had found for us. As he shook my hand, I mumbled something about appreciating his advice and all his help and I would keep him advised of Julie's status.

Rather than being turned off by Dr. Greenspan's warning, I was intrigued by the concept of patterning. After several months at home watching Julie propped up in her chair, staring at the TV, I decided to take a chance on this controversial therapy. I made an appointment to take her to Philadelphia to the impressively named Institute for the Achievement of Human Potential.

I borrowed my mother's car, packed up Julie and Linda, my new home health aide— who had appeared at my door one day saying the elevator man told her I was looking for a nurse—and drove to the northern outskirts of Philly for a week's stay at the Institute. I was interviewed, Julie was examined, and I spent the next several days in a lecture hall with the other parents, learning about the human brain and how crawling was the key to a child's neurological development. Then we were taught the basic patterning exercise. We were told that this concentrated crawling movement exercise would become imprinted on our child's brain and neurological system and stimulate neurological growth. I was given instructions on how to build the padded table on which we'd pattern Julie and also the crawling slide on which she soon would be able to begin to move. Then I was handed the hourly schedule of patterning, breathing, and crawling that needed to be adhered to each and every day of the week. By the end of the week I was hyped on this new therapy idea and couldn't wait to get home and start recruiting the many volunteers I'd need to carry out the program.

In spite of all the miracle stories I was told and the positive vibes from the enthusiastic staff, I had no illusion that Julie would ever regain all the brain cells that chemotherapy and radiation had destroyed. But it seemed possible that patterning could help her regain some movement, make her easier to care for,

and give her a chance to enjoy more of life. And with movement, any movement, we might be able to find a way for her to communicate. I grabbed onto
this therapy concept as the only chance Julie had, and vowed to go with it no
matter how far-fetched it sounded.

The basic patterning exercise involves three or four people moving the
child in a crawling pattern, one to turn her head, another to move her right arm
and leg forward in a crawling movement, as a third, moved her left arm and leg
in the counter movement. If the child is very stiff or large, another patterer is
needed at her feet to help with the leg movements.

I began to plot out the schedule and was shocked to realize I needed to find
fifty to eighty volunteers for the week. As I tried to calm my panic at this daunt-
ing number, I started to devise a recruitment plan. My first step was to put up
a sign in my apartment building mailroom and in a few other large buildings in
my neighborhood.

Volunteers Needed
Please come and help a nine year old in an exercise program
Work in a group of four – one hour a week
No experience needed

I was amazed at how quickly the phone began ringing. Within a week, our
apartment was a hub of activity. It felt as if I had opened a window and fresh
air was blowing in. I became energized with this new endeavor and all the
people coming and going. And Julie was not alone anymore. She had a network
of new friends teaching her, moving her, motivating her, laughing with her.
She seemed to love being touched and moved by her new friends, often ahhing
with pleasure. I saw her blossoming with all the activity around her, and with
meeting, recruiting, organizing and then teaching everyone to do the program,
I blossomed, too.

I couldn't get over how quickly our lives had changed. Our apartment,
into which Stu and I had moved when I was pregnant and where I stayed
when we separated, was in a very large building on West End Avenue. I hadn't
known many people beyond my floor and the parents of children Julie's age
whom she had played with in the playroom and in Riverside Park. First I got
calls from several of these parents and from two people on our floor. Then I

got calls from people I didn't know, more women than men. The women who responded could not be categorized, but the men who did come and who did stay on to become patterners were mostly teachers or social workers. An exception was Jeff, from the other wing of our building, who was in the middle of a custody battle with his wife. He was an attorney and thought that becoming a volunteer might cast him in a good light with the judge.

My mother, now in her late sixties came in on the subway from Queens once a week, with her neighbor Lil, making three changes of trains. And my sister Joan came one evening a week with her law partner, Marcia, and brought into the group some attorney friends whom I also knew; these then brought their friends. The conversation over Julie's patterning table was very legal on those evenings. Julie always greeted her Auntie Mame with a beaming smile and often couldn't stop ahhing and giggling when Joan called her Patrick.

A woman judge friend of my sister's also began to come, and when she couldn't make it she sent her twenty-year-old son. The first time, he was so nervous and emotional about what might be in store that he immediately went into the bathroom and threw up. But he did stay and was won over by Julie's smiling and giggling attention. He came back several other times for his mom and then on his own.

And Stu came. I think he found it easier patterning, than when he just visited, sitting on the couch next to Julie and trying to get a response. Sometimes he even came with his new wife. As time went on, after they divorced, he found the patterning table fertile ground for dating prospects, as did several other patterners, two of whom met over Julie's table and eventually married.

Some patterners became close friends as well. We'd go to dinner, sit and watch TV, and talk about things other than patterning. I began to feel I had a caring support system, a new kind of family. I had been dating a friend of a friend whom I got to know when I was with Kim. As I met more patterners even my dating pool expanded. I briefly dated two women whom I first met as patterners. Both were lovely and sweet and also really cared for Julie, but I was not in love with either.

I put signs up in the bookstores that dotted upper Broadway in the seventies and early Eighties, in neighborhood health food stores, gyms, on the bulletin boards at Columbia and Fordham Universities, and in the synagogue newsletter where Julie had attended nursery school. More and more people joined what was beginning to feel like our extended family. The world was coming to Julie. Her patterning table became the center of the universe for that hour. It was the equivalent of the quilting bee circle or the general store. The first few years we worked eight-hour days with four one-hour patterning groups, and an hour rest in between. During the rest periods, not taken up by lunch and dinner breaks, we either read to Julie or showed her word cards. At full steam, we had over eighty people coming each week. I made a large cardboard weekly schedule listing patterners' names and phone numbers. Some of the patterners helped with the scheduling and finding substitutes. As I got bolder, I called university physical therapy programs and was invited to speak to students about patterning and offer them hands on experience in this new and controversial program. Then I called some private high schools and touted Julie's therapy sessions as possible community service experiences for their students.

The more volunteers we attracted, the more I realized that the people who came to help Julie were getting as much from their volunteering as we were from their service. What at first I thought would be a difficult chore became less forbidding with each phone call and each new encounter with this new world of amazing people who became part of our lives.

Once we started patterning, the house was filled with energy and light, and the days flew by in a blur of people coming and going. But every night, when the last patterning group left and I kissed Julie good night after Linda readied her for bed and went home, I was alone with all my doubts and fears about what lay ahead. I needed to find a safe place where I could unleash my worries and take care of myself emotionally. I found this haven in a special kind of therapy called Primal Scream, which my last acting teacher had recommended when I told him about Julie and that I was leaving class.

Primal Scream therapy reminded me of the song-and-dance acting exercise. Each week I went to the therapist's office and sat in a circle with the three others in my group session. When my turn came, with coaching and caring touches from them, I began to take deeper and deeper breaths into my abdomen until I connected to a spot deep inside my chest where I was holding onto my pain. Then I opened my mouth to the scream that was being released. I screamed and screamed each week for over a year and was always amazed there was more screaming left each time I came back and sat down in that special circle.

As time went on, patterners came and went and new ones took their places. Julie had come home from Rusk with a feeding tube in her stomach, as she had lost the ability to chew or swallow food. Also her head drooped forward like a newborn baby's if not supported, and her arms were pulled up tight at the elbows against her chest, with her fingers often clenched into fists. Although she was alert at times to what was happening, making giggling sounds when she was pleased or happy and crying sounds when she was upset or in discomfort, there were many times she was groggy and uninvolved with the world around her.

But by the end of the first year of patterning, as Julie turned ten, she had vastly improved her ability to hold her head up on her own ... **and** she also recovered a gag reflex, enabling her to chew soft foods and swallow thick liquids. We all celebrated the day her stomach tube was removed and relished in her delight as she tasted food again.

Around this time, I began to think that I had wasted my younger years in a frivolous dream of being an actress. The only career that made any sense to me now was to become part of the helping profession. I made the decision to go back to school to earn a Masters in Psychological Counseling. With some planning I was able to fit most of my classes around our patterning schedule, with Linda running the few groups I missed each week.

As the second year progressed, Julie continued to improve. She gained more control over her head and neck muscles, and her arms and hands gradually unlocked into a more natural angle. As the pattern became imprinted in her brain, she became looser and easier to move during the patterning. Soon we noticed some spontaneous leg movements up and down when she was lying on the table between patterns while the group was talking with her or showing her word cards. Also we saw her beginning a basic cross pattern crawling movement when she was placed on the twelve foot low angle slide after each pattern. As the pattern sessions continued, we watched in awe as her ability to carry out this crawling pattern herself on the slide progressed. She was now moving her head from side to side as she pulled herself forward and using stronger arms and leg movements. Soon she was pulling herself forward and down the entire twelve-foot slide to the cheers and applause of her ecstatic patterners who shouted "Turn your head. Pull your arm back. Dig your knee in..." as she went along. When she reached the bottom, I always enjoyed her lifting her head to watch closely as the coins she earned for this feat were deposited into her money jar.

The four patterning groups a day, interspersed with the reading and teaching exercises, were aimed at keeping her mind active. I kept hoping and watching to see her begin to control her eye movement so we could establish some form of communication system. The two morning groups were filled with retired people, teachers on sabbatical, freelancers, and actors between jobs. During these groups, Julie heard tales of loneliness, illness, foreign travel, doctoral thesis, audition traumas, and personal relationship details–sweet and sour and sometimes sexual. The afternoon groups were mainly teenagers. From these, Julie, who was nearing her teen years herself, learned of parental disagreements, drinking, drugs, first love, and sex again. The evening groups had people straight from work bursting with events of the day. Some of these evening volunteers came in tired, but during that hour with Julie, I watched them become energized and happy to be there.

The apartment filled with more and more equipment as Julie gained movement and the exercises changed. At one point, to help stimulate her head control, we hung a cushioned wicker chair from the ceiling and slowly spun her one way and then the other. Another time we had a hammock stretched across the length of the living room windows in which to rock her between groups to stimulate her other senses. This hammock was a great hit, used often by any and all who visited. I especially loved to stretch out in it at the end of the day and slowly rock myself into relaxing as I watched the stars above and the lights in apartments across the street.

Some nights I couldn't stop crying for what had happened to my child, as I replayed over and over those early days in her treatment. Why didn't I stop it before it poisoned her? Why didn't her doctors know at what point the chemo had killed her cancer? If only they had stopped it then, she would be a walking miracle instead of what she was now.

thirteen

I taste a liquor never brewed
Emily Dickenson

One night in 1978, around nine, after the last patterning group left and Julie had been tucked into bed, I hurriedly changed from a baggy tee shirt over my jeans into a more form-fitting pale yellow V-neck sweater. I was applying blush to my cheeks and a touch of coral lipstick, when the doorbell rang. A woman I had dated briefly and with whom I was still friendly had arranged for me to meet someone she knew from her pre-med program at Columbia University, because "you are absolutely perfect for each other." I was intrigued hearing about this potential date who had left college to pursue an acting career and now, in her mid-thirties was fulfilling her dream of becoming a doctor.

I blotted my lips and took a deep breath before opening the door to greet a very attractive and self-assured woman about my height with shoulder length blonde hair that she tossed back with an air of sophistication. She smiled and said, "Hi, I'm Terri." I smiled back attempting to breathe naturally and nodding a hello, motioned her to come in. She was wearing tapered black jeans, heels and a flowing white silk blouse that was provocatively open to her cleavage. She was also wearing a vibrant pink lipstick. As I took in the sight of this lovely woman, I realized none of the other women I had dated ever wore lipstick. I also remember thinking I'd never dated a blonde except for a brief fling with that guy in summer stock in New Hampshire. And she was sexy; sex seemed to emanate from every inch of her being. She sat down on the ottoman. I poured wine for both of us and sat down on the couch across from her. We talked about her plans to go to medical school and I told her about Julie and the program we were doing and my new career plans. As we talked, I felt my heart racing and I knew I was falling in love.

A few months later, Terri gave up her sublet and moved in with us. By this time we were a couple, and she had won Julie's heart as well. Six months later, when she completed the pre-med program at Columbia, she applied to medical schools but was not accepted in a U.S. program. She was however accepted in an accredited program in Guadalajara, Mexico.

As our relationship deepened, our impending separation loomed before us. Our first taste of being apart was when she went to Mexico for a six week immersion course in Spanish so she'd be able to understand what she was learning when she began her studies.

In June 1979, I completed my Masters Program and my six-month internship assisting the rehab counselor in Columbia Presbyterian Hospital's Department of Rehabilitation Medicine. During my internship I knew that this was where I wanted to be, working with disabled adults in a hospital setting. But for my first job, I accepted a part time position in a city program focusing on unemployed minorities. I was still involved with the patterning when I was home but was turning more of the running of the groups over to Julie's caretaker and our volunteers. And now that I was earning money, I felt an enormous relief. I could end Stu's monthly ritual of coming by with his check for the rent. I never got used to accepting what felt like a "handout." However I was grateful that Julie was covered under his health insurance as long as he remained at ABC, as it reimbursed me for her medical expenses and helped toward her nursing care.

For the next two years, at the end of each trimester, Terri flew home for a few days. In between her visits, I left Julie with her caretaker and flew to be with Terri in Mexico City or Guadalajara. And when I was home, we burned the phone lines nightly with our calls. For most months of the two years, I never received a bill for those calls. I imagined there was an operator somewhere listening in to our love talk, and in return doing us the favor of wiping my long-distant bill clean.

When Terri finally completed the first two years of Medical School in Guadalajara, she applied for an internship in the United States and was accepted at a New York hospital. She went back to Mexico only to take pivotal exams. Aside from her seventy-two hours shifts each week she was home with us. We were together in what felt like a marriage, and Julie was an integral part of this relationship. As time went on, the patterners got to know her. Some, like my mother, accepted her as my roommate; others saw she was my partner and Julie's other mother.

Terri introduced me to the lesbian social scene. In the seventies and eighties, there were a stream of bars and dance halls specifically for women, where we could meet, have a drink, and dance in a safe and in some cases even an elegant atmosphere. I loved going out on a date with Terri—having the chance to put on a new blouse or slacks, then standing in front of the mirror together while we put on our going out make-up–mascara, eyeliner, blush, lipstick—in anticipation of the evening ahead. My favorite locale was The Sahara Club, a very chichi bar and dance hall in the East Sixties, run by four women. And then there were bars like the Duchess, in the West Village, where we could be comfortable sitting in jeans at the dimly lit bar.

Terri doted on Julie and treated her as if she were a normal teen. When I came home from work one day, there were Terri and Julie in front of the hall mirror. Julie was sitting in her stroller chair draped in a fancy flowered shawl, wearing earrings, a flower in her hair, and a pair of high-heel black shoes. Terri was in the midst of applying rouge and lipstick on her. I began laughing and crying at the same time as I saw the joy in Julie's watchful eyes as she saw herself in the mirror being made-up.

One day I got a call from the woman who was the supervisor of Rehab Counseling at Columbia Presbyterian Medical Center, under whom I had done my internship, telling me she was retiring and asking whether I would I like to take over her job. I jumped at the chance to fulfill my dream of working in a hospital, and a month later found myself counseling patients recovering from an injury or illness which might alter their ability to return to their previous lives. My caseload was very mixed: young men suddenly paraplegic from a gunshot wound, a woman experiencing the progression of her MS, an attorney with residual paralysis and speech problems after a stroke, a diabetic truck driver, who'd had a partial leg amputation. I was excited and filled with ideas of how I could be of help to my patients. I felt I had truly turned the page, leaving my acting career behind.

I was in love, Julie was still making gains, the patterners were still coming, and I was starting my dream job. I felt truly happy and was always surprised when friends offered me their sympathy.

fourteen

Amazing grace how sweet the sound

John Newton

We continued to pattern Julie. The signs I posted changed from *"9-year-old to 10, then 11,* then *teenager.* They stayed teenager, as I thought it wouldn't give the correct impression of what to expect if I wrote, *"Please come and help a 20-year-old in an exercise program."* Julie had stopped growing and stayed looking like a young teen the rest of her life, never weighing more than sixty or seventy pounds—which made it easy to lift and carry her.

Linda was Julie's primary caretaker for ten years and became part of our family during that time. We saw her four children grow up and she become strong enough to leave her abusive husband. When she went back home to North Carolina to marry a childhood sweetheart, I again asked our elevator man if he knew of a home health aide who was looking for a job. Lynette knocked on our door a few days later, and from our first meeting I knew she was Linda's successor.

Julie was eighteen when Lynette, a singer in her church choir, became Julie's caretaker and "Amazing Grace" became the starting song for each of the four five-minute patterning sequences in the hour. By this time we had replaced the one dimensional patterning table with a turtle shaped canvas vest, suspended from the ceiling, in which Julie was placed with her arms and legs hanging free to the force of gravity as she was patterned.

Lynette's voice rang out above the others as she began each pattern by turning Julie's head to the right, signaling the left side person to pull Julie's arm and leg forward, while the right side person moved her arm and leg back. As soon as Lynette began singing, we could feel Julie's limbs unlock, allowing us to move her more easily.

After "Amazing Grace," different patterners contributed their own favorites, and depending on their ages, Julie got a tour through musical history. I always chimed in with "A your adorable, B you're so beautiful, C you're a cutie full of charms," one of the songs I sang to her each evening in our rocking chair before she got sick.

Every five or six months, we returned to the Institute for evaluation and new ideas to enhance Julie's patterning program. As some of our volunteers became more involved they asked to come with us to Philadelphia. I welcomed the company and the help, as it made my status as single parent less burdensome. A few times, Terri was able to get time away from the hospital to accompany us. The staff at the Institute were hard taskmasters. Many times, it felt as if I were being patterned as well as Julie. The rebel in me did not like to be called to task for not completing a piece of equipment in time or for Julie's not meeting her goals, even though I knew they had her welfare at heart.

I was so thankful I had not listened to Dr. Greenspan. But he was not alone in his thinking. I kept running into the same objections against patterning whenever I took Julie to a doctor. They repeated Dr. Greenspan's warnings as per the dictates of American Board of Pediatricians. Once we embarked on patterning and I saw how much it helped Julie and nourished our life as well, I took on the role of crusader every time I encountered an MD who quoted the American Board of Pediatricians objections, which I knew firsthand were illogical and not based on anything I encountered or experienced.

The families I met told me that instead of breaking up their family, doing the program brought their family closer together by helping their child or sibling. I saw parents who first came to the Institute for training without their other children, return with them for subsequent sessions because they refused to be left out of the process.

Parents who came to pattern Julie laughed at the pediatricians' other point: that it was cruel and abusive to move a child against their will, and that the handling by others in this process caused bruises and other harm to the child. They told how often their own kids got bruises from climbing in the playground or falling off their bikes.

Julie did get bruises at the beginning because her skin had not been touched for so long and she was frail from not moving. I was overjoyed to see her knee get calluses from crawling, and see her eyes sparkle with enjoyment when she was moved and spun and exposed to stimuli. I loved to be part of a group as she giggled and made sounds along with the patterners' jokes and banter and songs as they moved her. Her interchanges with her now friends were as close to playing as anything I could imagine for her.

Julie's illness affected everyone's lives we touched. Most friends continued to be supportive and helpful, and many became patterners. But one family of a former playmate of Julie's was so unable to deal with what had happened to her, that whenever they saw me walking her in her stroller, they'd cross to the other side of the street and pretend they didn't see us. I used to fantasize that I'd follow and confront them, but instead I swallowed my hurt and anger and kept going. Another couple I knew who had originally decided to have only one child changed their minds and decided to have a second, just in case. And my sister throwing caution to the wind, now feeling it important to live in the moment, co-bought a house in the Springs section of East Hampton.

My sister, generous as always, offered me the use of her new beach house when she was not using it. I took patterners with us for the weekend, first with Linda and her kids, later with Lynette and her kids. We all relaxed in the sun, cooked on the grill, and even figured a way to do a modified pattern in the pool. We also rigged a life vest and rubber tire raft so we could float Julie around with us, splashing and turning her as she giggled delightedly. When any of our guests happened to meet my sister in later years, the first thing they'd say would be, "I've been to your wonderful house."

Terri turned out to be the perfect co- parent, helping me lead a full life with her as my partner; as well as pushing me to include Julie when we went to restaurants, the movies, even Broadway plays. Without Terri there as support, I would have avoided having to hassle with getting in and out of a cab with her stroller-wheelchair or finding a restaurant that was accessible. I still can see Julie sitting next to us in her stroller at *Cats*. At the dramatic moment when the cats realize the heroine is going to die and the audience gasps, there was Julie, wide-eyed, letting out a piercing ahhhhhh scream of sadness and understanding. When Angela Lansbury came to Broadway in *Auntie Mame*, Terri was at my side on Mother's Day as we took Julie and my mother to see the show. We sat in the fourth row center, with Julie in the aisle in her stroller. Julie started laughing in recognition during the overture and let out loud squeals each time a song she liked was sung. I kept thinking we would be asked to leave but no one seemed to mind.

From time to time Terri had bursts of anger that seemed to overwhelm her. During these outbursts, she sometimes vented her anger by throwing objects, once smashing a small wooden chair and another time a porcelain lamp. I was usually caught off guard and didn't know how to react other than to leave her alone to calm down, as she usually didn't respond to any intervention to help her refocus. My instinct was to leave the apartment, but I didn't want to leave Julie there alone with her. So I settled for just going into another room and letting her work herself down. Over the years we went to couples therapy several times, and each time this seemed to help our relationship and calm her outbursts.

Julie's hospital bed had been given away when we started the program. Her new bed became a plywood board with a thin pillow on which she was placed each night on her stomach, because The Institute wanted Julie as much as possible to be in a crawling position so she might move. We placed her board in our room next to our bed to keep a better eye on her during the night. She didn't move forward much, but did often move her legs up and down and turn her head. Julie seemed to enjoy waking up in the morning and seeing her two mommies looking down on her.

One morning when I woke up, her head was raised and she was staring straight ahead, completely rigid and unresponsive. I woke Terri, who saw that she was in "status epilepticus" and decided we should take her to the emergency room at the hospital where she was doing her internship. As we didn't have a car, I called my sister, who arrived half-dressed and with tears streaming down her face managing to get us safely there. A shot of valium did the trick and Julie was her old self. But this incident was the beginning of the gradually increasing seizures that would eventually erode first her alertness and then her consciousness.

When Terri finished her internship, she went on to do her residency while I happily continued working as a rehabilitation counselor. My life as an actress seemed a distant memory, and I felt no regrets.

One evening in the midst of a patterning group, Terri came home from her hospital with a little brown furry dog peering out from her coat. As I was about to say "Oh, no," she rushed to explain that when she was on her way to the subway, there was a circle of people around this little lost dog who was going up to each one of them and sniffing. When he got to her she just couldn't resist picking him up. She said everyone cheered and someone even put a token in the subway slot for her as she snuck him through the turnstile under her coat. I tried to stay firm, but he won me over as Terri sat at the bottom of Julie's slide with him and we all watched her crawl down in record time, keeping her eye on the dog and ahhing all the way. Max became part of our family that night.

As the years seemed to fly by, Julie's progress slowed down from those first big leaps forward to minimal changes. I always knew that Julie would never be normal again, although the hype and energy of the Institute staff was geared toward that goal, and when I was there for evaluations I couldn't stop myself from getting caught up in their expectations. But by the late 1980s, when Julie was in her early twenties, after more than twelve years of sticking to the program, I felt in my gut that we had reached our optimum point and stopped taking her the Institute. At the same time, I knew we had to continue doing the program on some level to keep her functioning and probably alive, and to keep me sane. We gradually pared down to one morning group and one evening group each day with assorted volunteers coming in between times to read or visit with her.

Terri's temper outbursts continued, occasionally triggered by something I said. One evening, after we saw Woody Allen's *Manhattan,* I expressed how much I liked it and Woody's honesty in portraying his characters. Terri vehemently disagreed with my assessment. As I attempted to defend my point of view, she flew into a rage, slamming her hand against a store window on Broadway. I was thrown by her unexpected outburst and upset with myself for not knowing how to defuse it. All I could do was ignore her screaming and walk quickly home ahead of her.

Many times an outside source ignited her anger. Crossing a street, she might become angry at a car that didn't stop to let us cross, and she would start banging the side of the car. Once, in a car, she became outraged at a vehicle that passed us on the road and tried to race after it until I demanded she stop and let me out. As the years ticked by, a voice in my head was telling me to end our relationship, but my attraction to her was so strong I kept ignoring my instinct and tried to believe things would get better. All we had to do was go back to couples therapy.

During her residency, Terri began to specialize in geriatric medicine and in 1988 was offered a position at my hospital, while I continued as rehab counselor a few buildings away. Observing her, I saw what an excellent doctor she was and what a gift she had for diagnosis. But at this point, after being together for ten years, her continuing bursts of anger had begun to sicken me to the point that I lost my desire to be with her. By now, we had been to couples therapy too many times for me to even want to try again.

The night Terri began a tirade in the kitchen and started waving a sharp knife in my direction, I knew a line had been crossed and it was time to make a drastic change. I suggested we each see our own therapist to help us figure out what to do. A friend of mine recommended someone she thought would be a good match for me. Terri opted to begin seeing the therapist of another friend of ours. We had gone out with that friend, accompanied by her therapist—a heavyset middle aged woman—several times. I was struck by the camaraderie and closeness they exhibited on these occasions and wondered how this played out in the therapist's ability to work with her professionally. I was concerned that because of our social connection, this was not a good idea, but said nothing. On the other hand, I was very pleased with my choice of a therapist and after just a few sessions, found myself talking more and more about the possibility of separating from Terri. I didn't know what Terri was talking about in hers.

It finally became clear that our once idyllic relationship was beyond repair when I got up early one morning and noticed a letter left open very conspicuously on top of Terri's pocketbook on the hallway chair. It looked as if it was left there for me to see, so I picked it up. It was a love letter from her therapist that made it clear that her therapy sessions were a fraud and that our relationship was over. In it, her therapist expressed her love for Terri and her concern that Terri might not have the courage to leave me. The letter ended with, "Remember it's not over till the fat lady sings."

I sat down feeling dizzy and nauseous and made myself read it again, and then again. I walked into the bedroom and saw Terri sleeping peacefully in our bed and Julie still sound asleep on her board. I dressed quietly, put Max's leash on him, and took him with me into Riverside Park and then down to the river. After walking a bit and trying to calm myself by taking deep breaths and watching a few small boats make their way up toward the bridge, I sat down on a bench and turned my attention to the joggers and the bike riders and the nannies wheeling their baby carriages and sipping coffee in the early morning sun. When I returned to the apartment, Lynette was already there caring for Julie, and Terri was just waking up. I walked into our bedroom, sat on the edge of the bed and looked at this stranger I had loved for ten years. As she opened her eyes, I numbly said, "Guess what? The fat lady has sung."

fifteen

After great pain, a formal feeling comes-
First-Chill-then Stupor-then the letting go-
Emily Dickinson

When I asked Terri to move out, she packed most of her things and took them to a small apartment she had rented near the hospital. One afternoon a few months later, when I had had enough of feeling anger and sadness on seeing her clothing when I opened her closet or a drawer, I packed up the stuff she had left behind to reserve her place, borrowed a car, and dumped the last two boxes of our life together in her new lobby. When I got back in the car, it did not help that Rod Stewart's voice was crooning on the radio: "I didn't know what day it was when you walked into my life." My heart did a somersault as I heard "our song," I made myself turn off his words before he got to "you're in my heart you're in my soul." I forced myself to focus on the road and felt empowered as I drove home, a heavy weight lifted. I was free to move on.

My biggest problem was how to help Julie understand and accept Terri's absence from her life. Each time she looked up at our bed in the morning or around the dining room where we usually gathered for meals, I'd hug her and explain that Terri had to move closer to her hospital but that she would still come and visit as often as she could. Sometimes, from the ahhhs she expressed, I thought she understood me, but sometimes all I got was a blank look. Julie's week continued to be filled with the abbreviated patterning sessions and visits from her volunteers, and I continued to go to work, hoping not to run into Terri, which always seemed to open the old wounds.

I heard about the Lesbian Herstory Archives, housed at that time in an apartment on the Upper West Side, and was motivated to volunteer there to continue my connection with the Lesbian community to which I now felt such a deep commitment. Every Thursday evening I walked up Broadway to Ninety-Second Street to be surrounded by interesting women and conversation and bookcases and bookcases of literature and memorabilia of the lesbian community. I became friendly with the woman whose apartment it was and who was the co-founder of the Archives. Her name was Joan, like my sister, and she became my dearest friend– like a second sister to me and a second aunt to Julie.

As I continued to spend time at the Archives, I met and dated several very interesting, and I thought, captivating women. But every time, within a few months, each woman revealed a flaw I knew I could not endure if we were to continue our relationship. One woman began to reveal her strong hypercondriacal personality as we spent more and more time together, and was even transferring her medical worries onto me and Julie. Then there was Jessie, dear Jessie, whose almost thirty-year age difference was at first rather a turn on. But this vast difference in age soon began to affect me as it penetrated my psyche. As I was sharing my what-was-I-doing-the-day-Kennedy-was-shot memories, it hit me: she had not even been born in 1963. The coup de grace came in my apartment one night when she said, "I want to take you to Radio City Music Hall for Liza Minelli's concert next week." I hugged her, saying "Oh my God, I'd love that. I loved her mother sooo much." She looked at me with her beautiful twenty-three-year-old year old face and asked, "Who was her mother?" I felt as if someone had splashed cold water on me. I looked at her and knew there was no way this was going to work. Jessie was a very sweet young woman and I cared for her deeply, but somewhere inside I realized that not knowing who Judy Garland was, symbolized the impossibility of us being in a relationship.

Two years passed. It was 1991. Julie, still looking like a pre-teen, was twenty-four. I was fifty-four, still working at CPMC and continuing the abbreviated patterning program at home, but by now I felt something was missing. I was meeting women, single women, straight and lesbian, who were adopting children, and I began to think about adopting a child myself. In addition, after a short fling with her therapist, Terri was in a serious relationship and in the process of adopting a child. Adopting began to fill my thoughts. I remembered how much I enjoyed being a mother and thought I did it well, and I began to dream of having another child. After all the years of not wanting to have another child besides Julie, now that was exactly what I wanted.

Once I decided, I moved quickly, exploring the various options:

Domestic adoption from an agency. When I found out I was too old to qualify for a child less than ten years of age, I began to think that maybe it wasn't fair to a child to have such an old mother. Then I rationalized that I felt and looked younger and I knew I'd be a great mother. Besides hadn't someone just proclaimed that fifty was the new forty?

I moved on to explore Domestic adoption from a private source. "No," I was told by an attorney. "You're probably too old for a woman to want to give her baby to you." When he said that, I realized that though I didn't want to adopt a child as old as ten, I also did not want to start all over again with a new-born. Foreign adoption, the last option, was my answer. I joined a support group for singles adopting and met with a social worker for the required home study.

Then I began my search for a foreign country from which to adopt. Because I was single, divorced, with a previous child, and over fifty, there were not many countries open to me in 1991. I never brought into the discussion any hint of my sexual orientation, which would have been another stumbling block. I began day dreaming of a girl around three years old.

The social worker who did my home study referred me to a facilitator who was having positive results finding adoptable children in Romania. I drove out to Queens with Jessie whom I was still close to, to meet him. She waited in the car while I went into his house. He said he was about to leave for Romania that week to complete an adoption and would search for a child for me. I was impressed that he did not ask for any money at that time, as I had been warned in the support group not to give anyone money up front. My fantasy of my new child continued that night. I dreamt of a little blonde, blue eyed girl whom Julie would adore. In fact the child I was dreaming of looked just like Julie's favorite doll, Elizabeth. When I called the facilitator a few weeks later, he reported that his trip had been harrowing. He had gotten the child out after much red tape, but he feared this would be the end of Romania as a source. Their politics had radically changed as stories of stealing babies for American families, along with exposes of the horrendous conditions in Romanian orphanages, were making headlines in all the papers; as a result, Romania was cracking down on foreign adoptions.

I moved on to a support group called LAPA (Latin American Parents Association), composed of parents who had adopted, or were in the process of adopting children from a Latin American country. Whenever they found a facilitator who completed three positive adoptions they passed on that name to their membership. I was given the name of a woman who had done just that with children in Peru. After I spoke with her, the blonde, blue-eyed little girl in my mind changed to a dark-skinned, black-haired, ebony-eyed child. She said she would look for an available little girl between the ages of three and five. A few months into the search, I heard from some parents, well into their adoption process, that the courts had shut down in Peru and all foreign adoptions were being put on hold because of a government crisis with the Shining Path rebel uprising. I heard about some couples stranded in Peru for almost a year, not wanting to leave their child while trying to negotiate with that regime.

With Julie at home, I crossed Peru off my list, knowing I could not leave the country for any long period of time. Then I heard that there was one very promising option still open: Guatemala. LAPA gave me the name of a facilitator there who had helped three parents adopt children. Her name was Sara and I called her that night. She spoke English well enough for us to communicate.

"Hello, Sara, my name is Leni Goodman. I live in New York. I was given your name by LAPA, and I'm hoping to adopt a little girl–maybe around three years old."

"Oh dear, that is a difficult age. Most mothers give up their child at birth. The older children are usually in an orphanage by then because they are considered unplaceable. But I will look. Don't worry. I will look." She asked me to spell my name and give her my phone number. My fantasy continued: I kept dreaming of a dark-skinned little girl as I waited to hear from Sara. About three weeks later the phone rang.

"Hola, Leni. I have two girls–one is five and one is three–who might be available for adoption."

My heart started pounding. I closed my eyes and pictured a five-year-old and then a three-year- old and tried to imagine which one would be right for me. I didn't know what to say.

"I would be interested in either one I think. What do you think?"

Sara said, "I think three years old is a better age to adopt. She can make a better adjustment at a younger age. And she is very *blanca*. So she will look more like you, perhaps. I have seen her on the street pulling groceries for many blocks to her home. I will speak further with her mother. I'm coming to Newark Airport to escort another child to a family next month and we can arrange to meet so I can get to know you better."

This sounded real. I could not stop thinking of my new daughter. Each day, whatever I was doing, I imagined doing it with a three-year-old there with me and Julie.

A few weeks later, Sara called to say she was coming, and I drove out to a motel near Newark Airport to meet with her. Sara was a very attractive, slightly overweight, dark-haired woman. We talked in that motel room for an hour as I told her more about myself and about Julie.

"I'm divorced and work in a hospital as a rehabilitation counselor."…"This is my daughter Julie." I showed her the best picture I could find of Julie, smiling and looking alert in her wheelchair. "Even though she can't move or speak, she understands everything." I didn't want to scare her but I did want to make sure she knew, and that my new daughter would know, about Julie and about how disabled she was. I also wanted to impress her with how I had the situation under control and what a good mother I would be to the child she found for me. I was hoping that somehow she would magically know how to match me with the absolutely perfect child.

Sara told me about the process ahead: the various steps that needed to be taken, attorney, court, and foster care fees, time frames for all the legal steps, and the documents I needed to have once she found an available child.

A few weeks later, she called me from Guatemala, saying the mother had definitely agreed to place her three-year-old child up for adoption, and she would keep in contact with me as the legal process progressed. I kept an image of a dark-haired, ebony-eyed little girl with *blanca* skin in my thoughts as I waited to hear more definite news from Sara. I also couldn't stop myself from thinking about the mother and what she must be going through, agreeing to give her child up for adoption.

I tried to imagine what it would feel like to give away my child. When Julie was in Memorial Sloan-Kettering, with every doctor advising me to put her into a nursing facility rather than take her home, there was no way I could even think of parting with her. The only answer I came up with now was that this mother loved her child so much she was willing to give her up so she could have a better life in America than she would ever be able to have there in the slums of Guatemala City.

Then, after what felt like an eternity, Sara called to say the mother had gone to court and signed the papers to proceed with the adoption. I felt a pang of guilt for being happy at this news but quickly forced myself to focus on what Sara was telling me about the next step. She said her mother, Ommi, was coming to New Jersey to deliver another child and I needed to arrange to meet Ommi in that same motel to give her my birth certificate, last tax return, three letters from people I knew to attest to my worthiness to adopt a child, a police clearance report, my marriage and divorce papers and my completed home study that the social worker had updated from Romania's requirements to Peru's to Guatemala's, and $6,500.00–half the fee for the attorney and the required foster care expenses. I was hoping that the mother would get some of the money to help her but was emphatically told, "No, that would be against the law." Later I heard she was given a TV set.

Up till then, I hadn't allowed myself to believe that my new daughter was really coming. I had even chosen not to go to Guatemala to meet her during the process. Guatemalan law, at that time, did not require the prospective parent to meet the child before the adoption was finalized in their court system. American law did, however, require that they meet before the United States would issue the American portion of the adoption. My daughter would be traveling to the United States with only the Guatemalan half of her adoption completed. Only after she had lived with me for six month, would I be eligible to apply to the Surrogate Court to complete her adoption. At that time, I'd have to submit a new home study testifying that I was a fit mother and appear in court with her as part of this process.

I was willing to go through these additional steps because I was afraid that if I met her before the final papers were signed, I'd be too upset, if her mother changed her mind, or the country changed their rules. I knew how disappointed I had been when the two previous attempts had failed, and that was before there even was an actual flesh-and-blood child involved. But the moment I received the first photo of her, in a faded blue dress with torn lace trim, her large, almond Oriental-shaped eyes wide open to the lens, I was hooked.

Now that I knew my child was actually coming, it was time to call my mother and break the news to her. I had told my sister when I first decided, and she was supportive, as usual, even having her law partner write one of my letters of recommendation. I took a deep breath, dialed my mother's number and braced myself for her inevitable balloon-bursting response.

"Lenore, Lenore, what are you thinking? At your age you should be looking for someone to take care of you. Why do you want to burden yourself with a child?"

"Mom, this is the right thing for me. This is what I want to do with my life. You want me to be happy, don't you?"

"What you need is a husband. Then I can rest in peace."

After seeing me and Terri living together for ten years, sleeping in the same bed, my mother was suggesting that I find a husband.

"Adopting this child will make me happy. I want Julie to have a sister. I want a child that I can watch grow up. Don't you want that for me?" My mother was never comfortable with my baring my soul to her. And I knew she wanted to continue not confronting my sexual identity.

"Does Joan know? Call your sister. Talk to Joan. She'll tell you don't need this responsibility."

"Bye Mom, I'll talk to you soon."

My life was on a new course. As part of this new course, I needed a larger apartment. I looked at several possibilities on the Upper West Side, but the minute I walked into the three-bedroom apartment in our building, with its sun filled expanse, I knew this was the home in which I wanted to start my new life with my two children.

It was going to be everything I wanted in a home. Walls would be knocked down so that rooms could flow into each other. Doorways would be opened up to accommodate Julie's needs. And my new child would have the most perfect room in the world. Space and light were abundant, which became even clearer as the renovations progressed. The closets seemed endless. I never dreamed that in a few years they would be bursting full with our lives. I enjoyed clearing out the closets in the old apartment. All the things I had saved for when I finally had a new space, I now pulled out and reexamined in the light of what I now wanted.

Sara told me the Guatemalan part of the legal process would take six months. All the time I needed to renovate, I thought. The first step was for the birth mother to place her child in a foster care setting and no longer have contact with her. Then there were three occasions she had to appear in court to verify that she was freely agreeing to place her child up for adoption. When I heard this, my heart sank. There was still a chance I might lose my child.

Sara arranged for Ommi to be the foster mother. My daughter-to-be left the slums of Guatemala City, where she had to get water from a pump down the street and sleep on the dirt floor of a one room apartment with her three siblings, with her mother in the bed nearby. She moved overnight to another world. Ommi's house was in an upscale section of the city. One of the pictures I was sent showed my new daughter lounging in pink flowered PJ's on an ornate gilt embossed chair next to a large TV set, holding a cordless phone to her ear. She now lived with Ommi, her husband, two grown sons, and a housekeeper. Sara, with her husband and two small children, lived nearby. She played with Sara's two daughters and was allowed to accompany them to their after school activities. She sat on the side of the pool, watching while they went swimming, but for some reason was not allowed to swim herself or attend school

What I did not know at that time was that her birth mother did the laundry for Ommi's family and continued to see "my daughter" throughout the entire foster care process. Her period of adjustment to their final separation only began when she tearfully said goodbye on the day she left with Ommi for her new home in America. She still remembers that her mother turned away and wouldn't say goodbye to her.

Finally the renovations on our new apartment were finished and the moving company piled all our furniture and boxes into the elevator to make their journey up the six floors to their new home.

When I wheeled Julie into her newly painted pink bedroom her blue eyes shone as they darted around. As I began to unpack her things and place them into the new drawers under her new dressing table she began to giggle, and when I placed her favorite doll, Elizabeth, on top, I saw by her smiling face that she knew we were in our new home. By noon Julie and I were completely relocated into our new home. The two children's bedrooms were connected with sliding doors now that the wall between had been knocked down, and their bathroom had pocket doors so Julie could easily be carried in and out.

The next morning, I awoke to the rising sun streaming into my bedroom and warming me in my new memory-free bed with its new flower-strewn cover. The bright yellow carpeting I had searched the city for was covering the floor, and my books and papers waited in boxes near my desk to be placed just where I wanted them.

sixteen

One sister I have in our house,
And one a hedge away

Emily Dickenson

My Spanish friends had warned me of "manana time" and the tradition of cushioning with double talk rather than ever being the bearer of bad news, which I soon experienced firsthand. Also I became educated in the unbelievable frequency of Hispanic religious holidays, which also closed down the courts. As six months stretched into seven and then eight, I now kept in contact with my attorney as well as with Sara and Ommi for updates on my new daughter. I went shopping and sent several sun dresses I thought she would like, some coloring books and crayons, and a cuddly stuffed teddy bear. I also put together a photo album story of me and Julie and Max, the dog Terri left behind when she moved out, including pictures of our apartment and neighborhood, so she could see where she was coming, and who her new family was to be. As fall turned to winter, I sent a cute blue and white sweat suit with a hood that I thought she'd need to keep her warm when she arrived. I was told that her name was Jazil but that she was always called Cache, which was a slang form of a Spanish word, something like *catchina* for "big cheeks" or "red cheeks," because she had large, round, red cheeks.

There were many late-night phone calls during those eight months of waiting. Sara's English was passable, but Ommi's was almost nonexistent so I had to arrange for a Spanish-speaking neighbor to be with me when I placed my calls. Once, when neither of my Spanish-speaking neighbors was available, I hijacked a night handyman from his post to translate for me. That was before I learned of the AT&T translator service, which, for a small fee, set up a three-way conference call with a translator on the line with us.

All my friends except one, whose husband was refusing to adopt a child with her, were cheering me on. I think my sister was having some influence on my mother, as her negativity seemed to lessen as the months progressed, in addition, I made it a point to never bring up the topic in our phone calls.

I also was getting great support and comfort from the singles parent's adoption group I joined and went to each week, along with Terri, whom I had reconnected with in our mutual search for a child. The members were mainly single women, but there also were two women couples who said they were just friends, and at one point there was a single man. The group was mixed between those who were just starting the adoption hunt, those in the midst of the process, and those who already had their children. Our meetings were divided between advice and comfort for those in process, and dealing with problems arising for those who already had their children. The children usually came to the meetings and the various holiday parties we held. Then I discovered a new group with the impressive up-front name, Upper West Side Lesbian Moms, a group of about twenty lesbian mothers living on the Upper West Side. These women, mainly couples but a few single women, had either born a child or adopted and met weekly to socialize and gain support from each other and for their offspring in the mainly heterosexual world. When I first called, I was told I couldn't join until my new daughter actually arrived, but when it came out in our conversation that I already had a daughter I was welcomed into their community.

When Sara called to ask me what name I wanted on my daughter's new documents, I felt as if my heart would jump out of my chest. I chose Cache as I thought that was the name she knew, and Elizabeth for her middle name, after Julie's favorite doll, so that she would feel connected to her new sister. Finally, after another delay from the Guatemalan court system, there was one more glitch on the day before Cache was to have left. I got a frantic call from Sara for me to call the United States Embassy in Guatemala City. The papers I had submitted gave my last name as Goodman, which I kept after my divorce as I was known by that name in my acting career. But according to Guatemalan law, a divorced wife could not retain her husband's name. So Cache's last name on her papers had to be changed to my maiden name, Ellenbogen.

I immediately placed a call to the US Embassy in Guatemala. I told the representative, "I don't care what name you put on her documents, just so she gets here." She laughed and asked me to fax her a corrected name document. The Embassy approved the new documents and my daughter was all set to travel the next day to Newark Airport, with Ommi as her escort. She would enter the United States with a birth certificate and green card with the name Jazil del Carmen Elizabeth Ellenbogen. I wondered what happened to "Cache" but didn't dare ask. I knew, that in six months, when we filed for the United States part of her adoption, I'd change her name to Cache Elizabeth Goodman and also apply for a social security card in her new name. Everything was ready. Then, unbelievably, that night Ommi's husband had a heart attack and died, and their departure date was delayed a few more weeks.

I had taken a crash course in Spanish at work and compiled a stack of index cards with appropriate greetings, loving phrases and day-to-day terms and objects I'd need in attempting to communicate with my new daughter. I'd pull them out from time to time and try to wrap my tongue around the foreign sounds, with remnants of my high school French getting in the way. I bought a taped Spanish program that I'd listen to when I was on the treadmill, and then respond to the instructor's voice in my ear. I also bought some beginning Spanish/English children's books, for me to learn Spanish and for Cache to learn English, and I taped an index card with the Spanish and English word on everything in the apartment.

Finally on February 19, 1993, a chauffeured car, courtesy of my sister, arrived to take me to Newark Airport to meet my new daughter. I brought Terri with me—who had recently come back from Mexico after completing her adoption of a year-and-a-half year old son. She was going to be my main source of communication, as she spoke excellent Spanish from her school days in Guadalajara. I also brought my close friend Joan, who also spoke some Spanish, but whom I mainly needed for moral support. They met me at my apartment. Terri had brought two large floating balloons, and I was carrying a warm ski jacket and a video camera. A stack of index cards were in my pocket, and clutched in my hand was the card with my Spanish greeting for Cache on it. I said goodbye to Lynette and Julie. Julie's face lit up, and she started to make loud ahh sounds when I said, "I'll be coming home with your new little sister."

There was horrible traffic on the way to Newark Airport, and I was on the edge of my seat worrying that Ommi and Cache would get through Customs before we got there. Finally we arrived and rushed to the gate. Even though we were late, we had to wait about ten minutes. Then I saw Ommi coming toward us. Her hand was on the shoulder of a little girl who was hugging the teddy bear I had sent her tightly against her chest. She was more beautiful than her picture, wearing a fancy green velvet dress with black ribbon trim and white Mary Jane shoes, which I later saw were a size too small. With them was a handsome young man who looked in his late twenties, rolling two large suitcases.

Joan started the video camera as I ran up to them, saying in my horrible French-sounding Spanish, "*Hola, Cache. Yo soy Leni, tu nueva mama.*" The little girl looked at me with a big smile and moved right into my open arms saying, "*Te amo mama.*" I was thrown by her greeting, wondering whether she had been coached to say this or whether this was her wishful thinking. My eyes filled with tears as I looked at her face, so open to connecting with me, her new mama.

I gave her the balloons as we walked over to Terri, who started to talk with her in Spanish. Ommi introduced me to her son, Coky, who was traveling with them and spoke English fluently. I invited them back to New York with us, but Coky said they would like to come the next day to say their goodbyes to Cache. I gave him directions to our apartment, and as unobtrusively as possible, slipped Ommi an envelope with the other half of the money. As I did this, an image of a 1940's espionage movie flashed through my mind and I was expecting an FBI agent to swoop down and arrest me for buying a child on the black market.

Cache was babbling away in Spanish with Terri and appeared to be enjoying her new adventure. I kept looking around for her luggage, but Coky didn't hand me anything from the suitcases, so I figured that they would bring all of Cache's things the next day. But the next day the only things they brought were the book of photos I had sent and a Guatemalan wallet and multicolored woven belt as presents for us. Where were the clothes and toys I had sent? Where was that sweat-suit outfit I thought she would need when she got off the plane in Newark? And where was her other "stuff?" Everyone has "stuff" don't they?

In the airport, Ommi and Coky kissed Cache goodbye and told her they would see her tomorrow. Then I bundled Cache up in the shiny new blue ski jacket and took her willing hand as we found our car waiting outside. Cache seemed at ease leaving Ommi and being with us, taking everything she saw in stride. With Terri translating, her first words in the limo were, "I want to go to school now. Can you take me to school?" She told Terri she'd been promised she could go to school in America and Terri assured her she'd be going there soon. During the whole trip back, she never sat still, bouncing on my lap, touching my clothing and face in between looking out the window at all the buildings and cars.

I used some phrases from my stack of index cards, and she looked like she understood some of what I was saying. But she continued to direct all her comments to Terri. When we got out of the limo at our building, I was thinking how different all this must be to her and watched her face closely as she drank in the people on the street, the tall building, and the doorman opening the door and greeting us. She looked fearless and happy as she walked into her new life. Holding my hand tightly, we all walked through the lobby and then into the elevator up to our apartment on the eleventh floor. Terri and Cache exchanged a few words as we made our way down the hall. I added a few phrases like *tu nueva casa*. Then I opened the door.

Lynette was sitting at the dining room table, with Julie in her stroller. Julie started to giggle when I introduced her to Cache. Cache had the most fearful look on her face at seeing Julie and turned to Terri, whispering what I later found out was, "What happened to her?" After all I had told Sara about Julie's condition, I thought Cache would have been prepared to know that Julie was in a wheelchair unable to move or speak.

seventeen

Cache, Julie and I were a family for five years.

Cache, hungry for a family, immediately adopted my mother, my sister, and my ex-husband as her family. I watched my mother morph again into an incredibly loving and caring and kissing grandmother to Cache, as she had been with Julie; far from the non-touching autocratic mother I had experienced. Her pessimism from before went out the window as Cache captured her heart completely.

Cache's lack of English didn't stop her from communicating any of her needs. She just took your hand and pulled you over to the object she wanted. As I fed her, I'd say the English words "milk, bread" and she enjoyed giving me back the Spanish word *"leche, pan"* as she pulled them out of the refrigerator. Her English grew by the day, as opposed to my Spanish, which remained minimal.

At first some English sounds were foreign to her ear—and her mouth. The *j* sound was particularly absent. Julie was Yulie for many months. I particularly loved hearing her say a word with an *r* as she pronounced that sound with a wonderful rolling of her tongue, which I would then try to reproduce, making her laugh. As she began to put words and sentences together in English, she retained a delightful Spanish accent. One day when she was struggling to find the words to tell me something in English, she stopped mid-sentence and said "I have so many stories in my mouth."

Two mothers in my Upper West Side Lesbian Moms group told me about a preschool program they were sending their child to in a church basement on Ninety-Third Street and Broadway that had a Spanish speaking teacher on staff. I enrolled Cache at Children's Underground a few weeks later when I had to return to work. Ommi had weaned her off the bottle and from diapers during the six months she took care of her, so she was readily accepted in the school. And I was proud to learn, from her teacher, that her proficiency in tying her shoe laces was a rare accomplishment for a three-and-a-half-year-old.

Just a few weeks after Cache arrived, Julie went into a prolonged seizure that looked like the status epilepticus she had gone into when Terri was with us. When she didn't come out of it, I took her to my hospital. This time a shot of valium did not pull her out of her frozen state and she was admitted. As the days in the hospital turned to weeks, with Julie not making any improvement, I resigned myself to stop fighting, accept her battle was over and that she was finally going to die. But I was devastated that Cache would be faced with losing her new sister.

Lynette, who usually cared for Julie and Cache while I was at work, was spending the days with Julie in the hospital. Terri surprised me by coming to the rescue, with an invitation to take Cache upstate with her and her partner and her son Mark. He was about sixteen months younger than Cache, and they became very close during that visit. She called him her god-brother. Even though I was trying to maintain an emotional distance from Terri, I felt it important for Cache to have this connection with Mark and we arranged visits and play dates for them for many years.

After Cache had spent a week at Terri's, I found a reliable Spanish speaking sitter for while I was at work and I was able to bring her home to her own room and to me. My department was just across the street from the main hospital, and I'd run over during the work day whenever I had a minute, to kiss Julie and try to get her to respond. But she remained unchanged, in her semiconscious state. One day Dr. Ryan, her neurologist, sat me down and said he didn't know what else to do to bring her out of her seizure and that I should plan to take her home. As I pondered the lunacy of taking my semiconscious child home, he wrote orders to discontinue all her meds. No medicine at all turned out to be what saved her. When I walked into her hospital room the next day, she was wide awake and giggled as soon as she saw me. She never returned to her previous state of alertness, but she was awake and she was my Julie again.

Over the next four years her moments of alertness and responsiveness slowly decreased. Nevertheless, we continued to do our abbreviated patterning program, because I didn't know what else to do. We still had a loyal group of volunteers coming to work with her and bringing life into our house. Now Cache was also here, bringing in more life and creating a relationship with Julie as well as with me. After her first shock of seeing Julie in the wheelchair, Cache became her closest companion, sitting on her lap as she was wheeled about, combing her hair, talking and singing to her, and soon helping with the patterning. She would stand in front of the leg person and help move Julie's legs forward and back as they recreated the crawling movement. She sang along with the patterners as they moved her, and then sat at the foot of the slide shaking the jar where the coins Julie earned for crawling were placed, encouraging her to pull herself forward another inch and then another foot.

The patterners, who were by now our extended family, also took Cache into their hearts. Those who spoke Spanish conversed with her and said her Spanish was on a very adult level as she asked them questions about their lives and families. When Julie first came home from the hospital, Cache told one of them that "Mommy is very sad and worried about Julie." And I thought I was doing such a great job of hiding my feelings.

Julie adored her new sister. She followed Cache's every move with her bright blue eyes. She listened when Cache spoke to her and giggled when she teased her, and also when I scolded Cache for misbehaving. Cache viewed Julie as her older sister, even though she was so completely disabled. She never tired of hearing stories of what Julie had done at her age, and she greatly admired Julie's artwork from earlier years, which was displayed around our apartment. Julie had been a prolific, and I was told, talented artist. Cache, at three and a half, aspired to do as beautiful art work as her sister when she grew older.

This new life was becoming normal—me at work, Julie and Lynette and the patterers at home, and Cache in school. Each morning I took her to school on my way uptown to work, and Lynette walked up there in the afternoon with Julie in her stroller and brought her home. Some days, Tia, a young Spanish-speaking sitter, whom Cache loved, would pick her up. As the months progressed, her English improved, still with a delightful accent. I assumed she would not lose her Spanish as she continued to learn a new language. But this was a delusion I had for a child wanting to assimilate in a home where her mother spoke English. She began to lose her Spanish, and as her English increased, her accent also began to fade.

As time went on and she felt closer and safer with me, she told me more stories of her life in Guatemala and how she had survived. One day, when she saw me pulling a belt through my jeans, she pulled my hand away from the belt and pantomimed someone raising a hand and repeatedly hitting the air, saying *mal, mal, mal nina.* I took her in my arms and repeated over and over. "No one is ever going to beat you again. I promise."

One morning after Cache had been with me about seven months, I was helping her get dressed for school, when she took my hand and pulled me over to her bed to sit down. Then she climbed into my lap with a very worried look and said "Mommy, I promised my sister to ask you if you could find someone to adopt her too." I remembered the pictures Ommi had sent of Cache standing with her sister and two brothers, but I don't know how or why I never dealt with the thought of their being left behind, and even more selfish of me, of what it meant to her to be separated from them. I silently kicked myself for being so obtuse. I held Cache close to me and said, "Oh my darling, I will do everything I can to make that happen. I promise." All day I kept hoping the hours would go faster so that I could call Sara. Finally I got her on the phone, and she gave me the news that Cache's sister, Debora, was already in the States as was her brother Pablo who had also been adopted. She gave me the names and phone numbers of the two families, but by then it was too late to call and I had to wait till morning. Sara also told me there was an older brother who was already a teen and too old to be adopted.

The next morning I spoke with Debora's new mother, Ila, a single woman in Wisconsin. She was overjoyed that I found her and wanted very much for the children to see each other and be a part of each others lives. Originally she had been told that Debora was six years old, but Debora had recently confided to her that she really was seven. This was confirmed by their doctor and dentist as well. I started to think that maybe Cache might also be older, but when I checked with her doctor and dentist, they both concurred that she was truly about four years old.

Pablo's parents lived closer by, on the south shore of New Jersey. They had changed his name to Michael and he was now five and a half, a year and a half older than Cache.

At first, they were concerned if it was the right time to open memories for him. They said he was still having difficulty becoming part of their family, still standing away in the back of the room whenever newcomers visited, wanting to take all his clothing and toys with him whenever he had to leave the house, afraid they would be gone when he returned.

Debora's mother and I planned a reunion at my apartment for the next summer. A few weeks before our reunion I got a call from another set of parents, also living in New Jersey, who said they had adopted a younger brother, Jose, now Matthew, born after Cache had left. They wanted him to know his birth family even though he had never met them.

By the summer, Michael's parents felt he was ready to be given the information about his sisters' whereabouts. When they told him, they said, he cried and confessed to them how worried he had been all that year not knowing whether Cache was all right and where she was and now was so happy that he would actually see her again.

When Debora and Michael and Cache first saw each other, there was a moment of awkward hellos. Then they fell into each others arms and didn't let go for a long time. All of them now spoke English with no trace of an accent. Cache wanted to show them her room and they disappeared into it, with Debora taking Matthew by the hand, while we parents got to know each other in the living room. Later that afternoon, we all went to Riverside Park. We sat on the benches along with the other parents and nannies, while our children ran and played together on the slide and swings. Watching them, I thought they looked as if they were one big happy family.

Debora, Michael and Cache shared stories about their older brother, Francisco: how he stole food from their plates and money from them on the street. Months later, Debora's mother told me Debora had finally confided that Francisco had tried to rape her and Cache; but he stopped when she kicked him and Cache scratched him with her long fingernails.

After that first reunion, I made it a point to keep in contact with Cache's siblings. At least once a year Debora came to stay with us over a school holiday, and when Cache got older, she went to visit Debora and her Mom. It was easier to keep in touch with Michael and his family, as they lived nearby on the Jersey shore. At least once a year his family brought him to the city to spend the day, or we drove down to visit with his family. Sometimes during the summer Debora joined us. At those times Matthew joined us as well. For several years, each time Cache saw or spoke with her older siblings, she plied them with questions about Carmen, their birth mother, and also about who her father might have been. Neither Debora nor Michael wanted to see Carmen again and didn't want to even talk about her. They also reminded Cache who her father was and how mean he had been to them. I tried to get information from Sara about who her father was and where he might be now, but she insisted she didn't know anything and couldn't find out anything either.

Debora remembered holding and comforting a crying Cache at night when Carmen was out. And she and Michael both would find places for Cache to hide when Carmen was coming to hit her. One day Cache and I took a train to the Bronx to visit some friends from our Single Parents group. Our subway train started underground, but as it went uptown it suddenly emerged out of the tunnel into bright sunlight on an elevated track. Cache was wide-eyed, looking out the window at the rows of houses almost within reach. As we passed a group of old tenement houses with open roof spaces, she pointed at one and told me of running up to the roof apartment of their building and being hidden from her mother by the woman who lived up there.

The safer she felt with me, the more she told me about her life in Guatemala. I listened, often in horror, and all I could think was thank the gods above that I had taken her from that life. I hadn't yet realized how much of her old life she carried within her.

Cache's Journal entry
(written when she was 14 years old)

I was born June 4, 1989 in Guatemala City into a family who had almost nothing, except each other. I had two older brothers and an older sister. Pablo and I had the same father, except he left after he found out my mom was pregnant with me and took all the money we had, which was very little, with him. We lived in a small building, in one of the poorest parts of the city. It looked like it had been there for ages. Parts of it were starting to crumble and fall off, so there were holes in it. The building, which looked like it might have once been a reddish-brown, was now just a dull and dirty brown. The glass on the windows all were shattered or were not there at all. Some people had put plastic bags, cardboard, and rags to cover their windows. It was pointless because someone would always steal it in the middle of the night.

We lived in one room, the five of us, unless my mother had a lover, and then he would be there also. The room was really small. There was a black stove in one of the corners near the door and on the floor around it were old used pots and pans. In the back of the room in another corner was a cot with a torn mattress on it, which is where my mother would sleep and often one of the many men. The rest of us slept on the hard and cold dirty floor, using each other as our pillows and torn clothing or dirty rags as blankets and sheets. Francisco sometimes was allowed to sleep on the cot, if one of my mother's boyfriends wasn't over, because out of all of us she loved him best—maybe because he was her first born. Maybe that is why she didn't give him up?

From the time we could walk, we all were sent out into the streets to beg, steal and wash cars for money. Michael, Debora and I would usually stick together because we were scared to be by ourselves. Except me. I didn't mind so much being alone. I liked being away from all the chaos at home and I enjoyed walking around by myself. Sometimes people would stop me to ask if I was lost or needed help. I would just look at them and give them a big smile. My sister remembers that's all I had to do to get money. She says I was the one who made the most money because I was so cute and friendly to everyone. I'm not like that anymore though.

Even though we would come home and give our mother all the money we made, she would flip out and start beating us with her bare hands or with whatever she could grab. And yell "this wasn't enough" and we were "good for nothing," And then she would send us back into the streets again. If we came home with nothing she would beat us even more and sometimes make us sleep out in the street. If she was really mad she would send just one of us outside to sleep because she knew that scared us the most. We didn't want to lose each other because that was all we had and she knew it.

Debora and Michael were the ones who took care of me. They were the ones who would protect me, when they could, from our mother. When my mother was beating Debora, she would glare at me and tell me I was next. Then Michael would grab me and start running like crazy down the dark streets around our neighborhood. I can remember us running down those streets.

And if I close my eyes I can still feel how the pavement seemed to move under my running bare feet, and I can hear the sound of the cool wind in my ears, rushing by as we turned the corners. I can still feel the rapid movement of my heart beating in my chest and how scared I was that my mother would come after us and do something even worse.

eighteen

Cache spent two years at the Children's Underground. By the time she left at age five, her ability to speak Spanish was completely erased along with her Spanish accent. In fact she now sounded exactly like me, except she could still roll her *r*'s.

Cache's life so far was filled with families similar to herself, as I felt it was important for her not to feel different. We continued to go to monthly meetings and holiday parties at our Single Parents group, and each June we joined other adoptive family groups at a camp in Connecticut for a weeklong gathering of adoptive families. Cache's pre-school also had single mom families, adopted children, as well as three other lesbian families; although they each had two moms.

I attended the Upper West Side Lesbian Moms support group, where our children joined us for holiday parties and play dates. Until Cache moved on to kindergarten at our local public school, she believed that the norm was to be adopted in a one-or two-mom or dad family. At P.S. 199, she was surprised to meet kids who lived with both a mother and a father.

Cache seemed to be adjusting and growing well, and I was enjoying my role of mother to this young child, while also juggling my caretaker role with Julie and the patterners and my work role at the hospital. I was extremely happy and felt fulfilled for the first time since breaking up with Terri. I didn't miss my previous dating life or the fact that I didn't have a soul mate; which bothered my friends who kept nagging me to find a partner. At times Cache would ask me to find a man to marry so she could have a father of her own. When she realized she could not talk me into that scenario, she was very accommodating and changed her plea to wanting me to find a woman to marry so she could have two Moms, which in her mind, was closer to a real family than what she had with just Julie and me.

I was very conscious of needing to provide a father figure for Cache. I wanted to create as much of a normal family as I could for her to grow up in. A few of Julie's male patterners spent extra time with her, but Stu became the primary father figure. Whenever he came to visit Julie I made sure Cache joined them, and as she grew older he did make an effort to make her a part of his life, sometimes with sleepovers and visits with him and his current wife, whomever she was at a particular time. She also continued to have a close connection with my mother and sister. She was even calling my sister Auntie Mame now as she became the newest recipient of her generosity. One night, as I was putting her to bed after Aunt Joan and Grandma had visited us for a holiday dinner, she told me she had a new definition of what a family is. I sat on the edge of her bed and waited for this new revelation. Settling back on her pillows, she began:

"When you ask for a present, a mother is someone who tells you, 'Let's think about it.' A grandmother says,' Okay, I'll get it for you tomorrow' and an aunt says,' Guess what, I just bought that for you and I'll be right over with it.' "

After Cache had been in kindergarten for a month, I began to get reports from her teacher that she couldn't sit still or pay attention in class. I had heard this from her pre-school teacher but had assumed it was part of her adjustment to a new setting. But now I also began to notice she wasn't recognizing words the way I remembered Julie had by age five, constantly picking out words in the newspaper and reading aloud–"Don't walk." "Fire Alarm Box." "Sale"–as we walked down the street.

Cache's teacher brushed this off with, "English is her second language and it might take her longer to learn words." But when she advanced to the first grade and still could not read nor recognize the thirty first words that every child should know by age six, I knew this was serious, no matter what her teacher said. Added to this, her inattention was getting her labeled a trouble maker and lazy because she didn't do well on tests. Against the school's advice, I took her for psychometric testing. The results indicated that she had above average intelligence but had an attention deficit in reading and math, and that she was also hyperactive.

The school principal laughed at the test results, saying he had never heard of such a specific attention deficit, and anyway the Special Ed classes in his school were filled with behavior problems and would not be appropriate for her. A parent told me an experimental one on one reading program was about to begin. I pressured the principal into finding a place for Cache in it, and immediately, in that one on one setting, she began to read. When I was told this program was not being funded the next term I realized I had to find a more appropriate school for her.

An ex-girlfriend of mine taught at Manhattan Country School, which she said was used to dealing with students with "learning differences." On her recommendation, I transferred Cache to her school at the beginning of the second grade. Although she missed her friends at P.S. 199, Cache seemed to like her new school and her new teachers.

But at home I began seeing subtle emotional problems that didn't feel OK. Sometimes when I raised my voice, she shrank away and would climb into bed and not want to get up. She berated herself when she made a mistake. Once I spent a long time convincing her to get up and go to a party, which she thought she didn't deserve to go to. A few times I noticed she would automatically cringe, as if averting a blow, when I reached overhead to take a book from the shelf behind her.

By this time, she had told me enough stories about her life with her birth mother to make me realize these traumas from her first three years needed to be dealt with. I found a therapist, Ruth, and began taking her weekly. Ruth worked with Cache by playing games and having her draw pictures and tell stories about the pictures. She told me all of Cache's pictures and stories had to do with the children saving the parents from bad things.

One story was about parents hiding in a closet while the children answered the door and had to convince the police, who had guns drawn, to go away. Another was about a mother drowning and a child pulling her to safety. Ruth said it was important for me to help Cache now experience a childhood without responsibilities and worries.

Most of the time Cache seemed fine, making friends and adjusting well. But then, out of nowhere, she'd sink into a sadness I couldn't kiss or soothe away. It frightened me that I didn't have the power or tools to save her. A few times she told me she didn't deserve to live and wanted to die. One night, when I was putting her to bed, she told me she had placed the large rock we used to hold the hall door open on her chest to make herself stop breathing. As soon as she was asleep, I dumped the rock in the garbage disposal room. One time at a Club Med, where I took Cache on vacations each Christmas while Lynette stayed with Julie, she ran away from me in the dining room after a disagreement. I frantically searched for her all over the grounds and finally found her on a ledge of the balcony looking out onto the sea shore below. I climbed out onto the ledge and took her in my arms. In a low voice she told me she had been thinking about jumping.

Cache's Journal

I don't think there ever was a time when I was able to make my birth mother happy or please her. To be honest I don't remember a time when my mother showed her love for me or said she loved me, or even being happy with her. I only remember her beating me and throwing glass beer bottles at me .And her saying, "You are worthless…no one will ever want you…you are good for nothing…you will never be able to do anything right." No matter what I did or didn't do, it was never good enough for her.

One day I came home with what I thought was a lot of money. It was more than I ever had brought home before and I was pretty happy with myself. I thought she would be happy with me, too. Boy was I wrong. She slapped my hand so all the money fell out of it. Then she grabbed a belt and started whipping me with it. I tried to dodge the blows as I ran to the back of the room. She threw the belt down and for a second I thought it was all over, that she was done. But she wasn't. She started picking up the beer bottles that were lying around the room and began chucking them at me with all her strength. I still remember the sound of the glass breaking against the wall and falling to the ground. I still remember the stinging feeling of glass cutting my face, and feeling this moment will never end.

But finally she stopped and crawled onto her bed and fell asleep. I sat there crouched in the far corner of the room trying to figure out what to do to make it better. Finally I decided to clean up the mess, praying to God that would make her happy when she woke up. When she did wake up I went close to give her a hug hoping that would make it better. It didn't. She slapped me across my cheek, shoved me from her and walked away.

I think now, why every time she hit me would I try to do something else to please her and then try to give her a hug? It never worked but I kept doing it, hoping she would change. But she never did. Nothing ever did.

nineteen

As Cache began her second year at Manhattan Country, Managed Care came to Columbia Presbyterian and drastic cuts were implemented throughout the hospital. Our new chairman, hired for his fund-raising skills, called me into his office and informed me that "the hospital is no longer getting reimbursed for the vocational services and testing that you're providing and your position is being terminated." He pulled all 350 pounds of himself up to a standing position, signaling our meeting was over.

Holding back tears I asked, "Can I have some time to put together a plan to bring revenue into the department?"

"You have till the end of the month."

I called several other rehab counselors but found that the only departments now able to obtain funding were those who worked with a drug-or-alcohol related population.

My proudest accomplishment was that the volunteer department promised to continue utilizing the disabled volunteers I had recruited and for whom I had obtained transportation funding. Finally I just let go and accepted it was time to move on. I knew I would miss my patients, but I felt a relief as well. There was now one less pressure to juggle. I became reacquainted with the unemployment insurance office, which I had not visited since my acting days. And I now had all the time I wanted for my two daughters at home.

Over the next six months I kept my little family afloat by doing some psychometric and vocational testing for two psychiatrists and taking a short detour as a telephone recruiter for a drug company. My job was to engage a doctor or the secretary in conversation until they agreed to attend a dinner presentation of our drug product. The first few days, almost every call I made was a sell. By mid-week I seemed to lose my touch, or maybe I was now given the hard sell phone list. On Thursday, after a no-sell morning, I was called into the dreaded glass booth overlooking our phone bank and yelled at for letting a doctor off the hook too easily. When I left for lunch I just kept walking and never returned. The next week the unemployment office welcomed me back and reopened my case.

Then out of left field, Terri called and asked whether I wanted to be her office manager in the office she and another doctor had set up in Riverdale. She was willing to arrange my hours around my schedule at home. I couldn't resist the offer and crossed my fingers that I had separated enough from Terri to feel comfortable seeing her each day. So I began my new career. When Lynette arrived to care for Julie, I took Cache downstairs to the school bus, then hopped on the subway to Riverdale to sit behind a desk, answer phones, and manage billing and appointments from ten until four, four days a week.

I lasted almost one year as Terri's office manager. Then the doctor who was her partner in the practice insisted she hire someone who could give more hours for less money. I was angry at Terri for not holding her ground, but in the end she chose her partner over me. Emotionally this was the best thing to happen for me, as I was now completely over Terri for good.

A week later I was handed the best job possible. I had taken a chance and walked into the doctor's office on the first floor of a nearby building, not knowing she was looking for an office manager, and was hired after a two week trial. Now all I had to do was take the elevator down to work and the elevator up afterwards, and Cache could stop in to say hello when her bus dropped her off after school.

But things were not going any better for Cache at Manhattan Country School than they had been at P.S. 199. In spite of my friend's assurance to me that her fellow teachers were experienced and understanding of learning differences, Cache was constantly berated for her attention lapses and her learning difficulties. As I witnessed my daughter's feelings of being dumb and unable to learn being compounded every week, I decided to ignore parents who had advised me not to place my child in a Special Ed school because it would mark her for life. I now realized that being marked for life was far better than not being able to read or write.

I found the perfect school just three blocks from our apartment and made plans for Cache to transfer there at the end of third grade. She was reluctant to change schools again and leave her friends, but she agreed to give this new school a chance and start fourth grade there in September.

twenty

More precious was the light in your eyes than all the
roses in the world
Edna St. Vincent Millay

When I went into Julie's room that morning and saw her lying there, not breath-ing, she looked so relaxed and at peace that my only thought was, "Oh my baby, my dear baby, you are finally free." I am not a religious person, but as I knelt by her bed and stroked her beautiful face, I imagined she was up in heaven skip-ping and dancing in a field of golden daffodils as in the poem she liked me to read to her.

She was thirty-one chronologically but frozen in time as a child. The past year, all I could do was stand by, watching as her energy and attention contin-ued to wane and her bouts of momentary seizures followed by falling asleep increase.

The last few days, her mini seizures had increased dramatically, and I called her neurologist, Dr. Ryan, to tell him her condition and remind him of my decision not to ever take her back to the hospital. He understood and told me that if she died at home, I just needed a doctor to certify it, and I could bypass having to call the police and having an autopsy. I asked him to speak with Dr. Gordon, for whom I was working, as she was the one I'd call when Julie died. When she got off the phone with him she said he told her it sounded as if Julie was near the end, and he didn't know how she had lived all these years with the damage her body and brain had sustained. She put her hand on my shoulder and told me to call her when the time came.

That night, in my mind, I went through the steps of what I'd have to do. I made sure I had Dr. Gordon's home number in case it happened at night and the number for Riverside Chapel, a nearby funeral home where I had attended a funeral a few months before when a neighbor died.

Now, kneeling by Julie's bed, I had no tears. I just felt profound sadness and at the same time a peace and a letting go that I also saw in her relaxed body. I had already mourned her loss years ago, when I first was told she was going to die. That morning, with her actual death, I felt as if I was at last released from an emotional limbo I had been floating in for twenty-five years.

Looking back over those twenty-five years of life Julie did have in her wheelchair, hearing and seeing and understanding at some level, but unable to speak or move, I wondered if that was what she would had wanted and whether I had made the right decision to intervene medically. Or should I have taken off with her to a tropical island and enjoyed those last promised six months with her? Then I thought what my life would have been like without her. The relationships I made because she was here, the strangers who first came to pattern and then became family, the career changes I made, the person I grew into, the new family I now had with Cache. Who would I have been if I did not have Julie in my life all those years?

Then I thought of Cache in the next room. She was going to be nine in two months. God, how was I going to tell her? Finally, I forced myself to get up and open the sliding doors between their rooms. Cache was still fast asleep. I sat down on her bed and gently touched her arm to wake her. When I told her, she first looked stunned, as if she didn't believe me, then as it sank in, her eyes filled with tears and she pushed past my arms and ran to Julie's bed and tried to wake her. I sat with her on the edge of Julie's bed for a few minutes and then whispered in her ear that I needed to call Dr. Gordon.

I quickly grabbed the phone from my desk and dialed Dr. Gordon at her home as I went back to Cache's side. She said she would come to my apartment on her way to her office. Then I called Riverside Chapel. The man who answered the phone spoke in a hushed and somber voice, expressing his condolences and telling me he would send his staff people over to bring Julie to the chapel and that they would bring a death certificate for her doctor to sign.

While we waited for Dr. Gordon to arrive, I sank to the floor with Cache in my arms next to Julie's bed and started to sing our nighttime songs that I had always sung to Julie and continued when Cache joined our family. In the middle of "A You're Adorable," I heard Lynette's key in the front door and her jubilant "Good morning, Julie. Good morning Cache, I'm here."

When Lynette came into Julie's room and saw us there next to Julie's still body, she let out a deep moan and began to sob as she dropped to her knees next to us. I numbly filled her in on how I had discovered Julie this morning. Through her tears she tried to pull herself together and attempted to get Cache dressed. But Cache just wanted to stay near me and Julie and I let her. I still had the phone in my hand and realized I needed to call my sister and Stu.

The men from the funeral parlor arrived at the same time as Dr. Gordon. I stayed by Julie's side as she examined her and then went into the dining room to fill out the papers the men had brought. When the men began to move Julie to a stretcher and cover her over, I had to turn away to stop myself from screaming "NO." As they left, they told me to come to the chapel whenever I was ready.

My sister arrived, red eyed and unable to stop crying. She accompanied me to the funeral parlor where we picked out a beautiful, small-sized, white coffin and made all the funeral arrangements. Then she came back to the apartment with me and we began the painful task of calling people.

I didn't want to call Terri. Why should I call her? She had deserted Julie. But Cache felt Terri needed to know Julie had died. And with all her nine years of wisdom, clearly told me so. She picked up the phone and dialed Terri's number herself and told her when and where Julie's funeral was going to be.

As the room began to fill up at the funeral parlor, it became clear that it was not large enough for the crowd that was arriving, and the staff opened a back wall to expand the space. So many of Julie's patterners were there, as well as all of my friends and my sister's friends and law associates and even some judges, and Lynette's family and Dr. Gordon and her husband, and many familiar faces from my apartment building.

I asked the cantor from Lincoln Square Synagogue, who taught Cache's Hebrew school and whose children had been in pre-school with Julie many years before, to officiate. I heard later that he himself had lost a daughter, and he spoke eloquently and personally about remembering Julie. The passage he read from Jewish legend recounted a mother who did everything possible to keep her child alive. I spoke after him and recounted happy times and Julie's resilience and love of life. Lynette told me afterward that she had wanted to sing "Amazing Grace" but was afraid it would not be allowed at a Jewish funeral.

I didn't speak with Terri, just nodded to her. My sister told me afterward that Terri had come up to her and said, "I made a mistake. I should not have let Leni go from my office." My sister said she replied," You sure did make a mistake," and turned away.

Cache's Journal entry, April 29, 2004

Dear Julie:

I remember just about everything the morning you died. I remember waking up facing toward the wall under my yellow sheets. It was bright and sunny out. I woke up because mom sat down on my bed and when I moved my leg I hit her. I looked up at her and asked what was going on because from the time on my digital clock I knew I should have been at school by then. I didn't want to believe her when she said "I think Julie is dead." I crawled to the bottom of my bed and looked over into your room and I saw you, only it wasn't you. You were gone.

I was mad at you for leaving us and at the same time feeling so guilty because I kept remembering all the times that I wished you would just go away or disappear. I was angry at you all that year for leaving when already everything seemed to be going wrong for me. I was angry with God for taking you away because I didn't have a sister anymore. I was angry at the world for not having found a cure for your illness when you were younger. I'm angry that no one told me you were leaving. I'm mad at you for not making any noise that night to tell me that something was wrong. I'm angry that I didn't wake up, not even once that night. I'm mad that it happened at night and not during the day when someone could have done something to save you. I'm mad that you had to die alone, that no one was there to tell you that they loved you. I'm mad that you left me all alone, that you, too, went away. I'm mad that I had to lose someone else I loved and cared for. I'm mad that every April 29th I remember it is the day you died. I'm mad at myself for never having really let you go because then I would be betraying you. I'm scared to let those feelings go because then I don't know what's there once I do. Maybe none of you will be there, none of the memories of the times we were together, and none of your smiles, with your blue, blue eyes.

But that is something I've got to risk because I don't want to go on living like this. I love you and will always love you but for now it is goodbye until we meet again in the clouds, in a golden field of daffodils.
Love, Cache

twenty one

After Julie's death, there was one particular book Cache kept asking me to read to her: *Why Dinosaurs Die*, and I'd see her looking at it by herself, especially at night, just before she went to sleep. One day she came home crying from school "I must be a terrible person because I didn't think about Julie all day and Cantor Goffen had told me that Julie is not dead because you will be thinking of her, and she will always live on in your memory." All I could do was hold her tight and reassure her that Julie was always going to be somewhere deep inside her thoughts.

At night, Cache started complaining that she couldn't sleep, even after we harmonized on an extra verse of "A You're Adorable," because she missed hearing Julie's breathing. She had been asking for a dog and I kept telling her she had to wait till she was older. Max had died a few weeks before Cache came and I had not thought about getting another dog until she was older. But now, this sounded like the right time. I put out feelers to everyone I knew for a dog that didn't shed. A few nights later a friend called that her babysitter's roommate had found a stray dog on the street and wanted to find a good home for it. We went downtown to Chelsea to meet a straggly little white poodle and bichon mix, about a year old. When we sat down on the couch, he immediately jumped up and put his head in Cache's lap. As we sat there being interviewed by the babysitter, I started telling her why we were looking for a dog at this time. She immediately broke into a huge smile and said her roommate's name was also Julie and now it was clear to her that our Julie had sent this dog for Cache to have. Who was I to question that?

September came, and in the midst of our mourning and trying to move forward, Cache began the fourth grade at the Stephen Gaynor School. As reluctant as she had been about changing schools and having to make new friends, she took to this school after the first day, and each morning looked forward to going. After about a week, as I was walking down the block toward her school, she came skipping up to me, waving her arms and shouting, "I didn't know learning could be fun. I didn't know teachers don't yell at you." Problem solved.

Cache continued to see her therapist, Ruth, for two more years and it seemed to help. But as she was approaching puberty, she felt there would be more problems and Cache now needed to be working with a psychiatrist who could prescribe medication. Ruth did not handle the separation well and no matter how I tried to help Cache make the transition to Dr. Leon, she continued to feel Ruth had deserted her. But when we met with Dr. Leon, she felt Cache did not require an antidepressant at this age and that therapy alone would be sufficient. In the midst of my trying to decide what to do now, a traumatic event took place.

We lived in one of the safest buildings on the Upper West Side. We had doormen and elevator operators day and night, providing all the security and comfort imaginable. As Cache got older, she began to travel the elevators up and down by herself to get the mail or visit a friend on another floor.

By this time, Dr. Gordon and I had parted company, precipitated by her decision to get rid of her billing company and have me take on that task as well as the office management. I did not feel confident on the computer, and also, it would have required an additional day and a half in the office with no increase in pay. I firmly said "No thank you," and left. After I was back on unemployment a few weeks, my sister asked me to work in her office as a legal assistant. I insisted on trying it out for a month without pay to see whether I could actually be an asset to the firm. By the end of that month, I saw my that my psychology and counseling background was useful with the firm's clients, who were usually in the midst of a very traumatic divorce or custody issue, and I loved the opportunity of seeing and working with my sister five days a week.

Each morning I walked Cache to school, then hopped on the No. 5 bus to my sister's office. Once she turned eleven, I felt she was old enough to walk the three blocks and across the three avenues home each day. When she got upstairs, her job was to take her dog, whom she had named BB, for his afternoon walk around the block before she settled down with homework or TV. I'd get home from work about an hour later. After a few months, BB was having too many accidents on the rug, and I spoke with Cache about taking him for a longer walk. I even took him to the vet to see if he had an infection. Then I began to think maybe she was being lazy and not walking him at all, and I became more demanding that she fulfill her obligation of having a dog. On New Year's Day, as we were about to go to our yearly New Year's Day after-party at a friend's apartment, I asked Cache to walk BB before we left. She said she was too tired, but I insisted and she reluctantly put his leash on and walked out the door.

Fifteen minutes later, as I began to wonder why she was gone so long, she burst into the apartment pale as a ghost and crying. She threw off her coat, ran to her room, and crawled into bed, pulling the covers over her head. I followed her, to try to find out what happened. Finally the whole story came pouring out. For months, the elevator man whom she had always jokingly called Skunk, because of the shock of white hair down the middle of his black hair, had been touching her all over her body each time she got into his car. Some days he was on the other set of elevators, or it was his day off and she felt safe. On the days he worked, if she saw him first, she would sneak around the corridor and walk up the eleven flights. If he saw her, then she'd get on his car instead of waiting for the other car, because she didn't want to upset him. After all, he had been her friend as she was growing up, always kidding around with her and letting her push the buttons for the floors. His touches got more intrusive, and this time he had stopped the elevator at our floor and started to unzip his fly. She was so frightened that she dropped BB's leash and ran to our door. This revelation knocked the wind out of me, and my first instinct was to run to the elevator and choke him to death. Instead, I ran down the hall to my neighbor Tom's door. He was an attorney and he would know what to do. He immediately called someone on the co-op board, who told him I needed to call the police and that he would notify the building manager to make sure Skunk did not leave the building.

Tom said he'd call the police and I should just go back to my apartment to wait. Cache was still curled up in a ball under the covers. I lay next to her, rubbing her back until the doorbell rang. It was two policemen along with two EMS men.

I heard myself repeating what had happened, but when they asked to talk with Cache, I insisted they call for a woman officer to interview her. A tall, sleek-haired Hispanic woman in a police uniform arrived at our door about ten minutes later. She introduced herself as Martina Sanchez. She had large, smiling eyes and a warm, in-control demeanor. I brought her into Cache's room, where she was still curled up in bed in a fetal position. Martina sat on the edge of the bed, introduced herself, and in a firm and calm voice, told Cache that she was here to find out what happened and help make sure the man would never hurt her again. Cache listened, then began to uncurl herself and sit up a bit more on her bed. Martina asked me to leave them alone so she and Cache could talk privately. I asked Cache whether it was OK, and after a momentary look of panic, she nodded. Afterward, Cache told me she imagined Martina was Olivia Benson, the woman officer on *Law and* Order: SVU. When I came out of Cache's room, our super had arrived to tell the officers he had stopped Skunk from attempting to leave the building and was having him held in the conference room next to the office, where he was now on the phone with his union rep. The two police officers asked our super to take them down to him.

Even though Cache told Martina that Skunk had not raped her, the EMS men insisted they needed to transport her to the emergency room for an exam and rape kit. I protested, trying to avoid that ultimate invasion for my almost-twelve-year-old, but finally I gave in. We all went down together and when we got to the lobby Martina took Cache by the hand and walked her back to the conference room, where Skunk was already being interrogated by the policemen. Martina assured her the blinds on the windows facing the hallway were closed, so he could not see her. Then one blind was drawn aside by an officer for Cache to look in and confirm that that was the man who had assaulted her. After she did, Martina accompanied us in the ambulance to the Mt. Sinai emergency room and walked us directly into the exam area.

When a male doctor approached, I told him I wanted only a female doctor to examine my daughter. He nodded his understanding and we sat with Martina to wait for the new doctor. A crisis social worker introduced herself and wanted to talk with Cache, who turned away into my arm. When the female doctor arrived, she allowed me to accompany Cache into the exam room. She gently explained each step of her exam to Cache as I held her hand and tried to soothe her terror, but she cried through the whole process and I was furious with myself for not resisting more strongly.

While we were in the exam room, Martina connected with the assistant district attorney who would be prosecuting Skunk and made an appointment for us to go to the Special Victim's Unit the next day to be interviewed. When we were ready to leave, she flagged a cab for us and praised Cache again for being so brave. I held my arms around my daughter in the cab and when we got home she didn't want to let go of me for an instant. I held her in my arms, singing our songs, till she finally fell asleep. I didn't sleep at all that night.

The next morning, we went downtown to meet with the ADA in the Special Victims Unit. She explained the steps that would lead to Skunk's indictment, and Cache agreed to do anything necessary to convict him to make sure that what happened to her wouldn't happen to another girl. The first step was for her to describe exactly what did happen, while the ADA recorded her testimony on video tape that would be played to the grand jury. I was asked to leave the room during the recording, and I never heard that tape. Cache looked drained when she emerged and immediately ran into my arms. The ADA patted her shoulder and complimented her on her testimony, saying that if it ever had to go to a trial, she would ask the judge to let the taped testimony be heard rather than have Cache face him in open court.

A few days later, when the grand jury convened, we came back, and I was called in to give my account of what happened. I had seen this scenario on TV many times and once played the part of a juror in a TV show. But that didn't prepare me for the nervousness I felt actually sitting in a chair facing a group of strangers, several of whom looked as if I could have known them from Fairway or Zabar's, as I recounted, from my perspective, what happened on New Years Day. A few asked questions after my testimony about my and my daughter's previous encounters with the elevator man. The two policemen who first came to our apartment were then called in to give their testimonies. After that, Cache and I and the officers sat outside the jury room waiting to hear what they decided. Within an hour we were told they had voted to indict Skunk. The ADA told me she found two prior rape charges in his record but could not use them in evidence if we went to trial because for some reason they were sealed.

I was thankful Cache never had to testify at a trial, as Skunk pleaded guilty. He was sentenced to six months in jail and officially listed as a Level 2 sex offender, which meant that his offense was determined high enough and dangerous enough to pose a substantial danger to public safely; his information would be registered and available through the local police department and the Sex Offender Registry Board. He got out of jail two months early for good behavior. But the ADA made sure an order of protection was issued against his coming anywhere near our building or Cache for ten years. I raised hell with my building's board and was told they were now doing background checks on all employees.

Cache did not get off as easily as Skunk did. She had flashbacks of the events and was frightened to walk to school or back alone for many months because she thought he might be following her. Sometimes in school she was found hiding in back of the coats in the closet, and I was called to take her home. I had taken her to see Dr. Leon, who assured me she was experienced in this type of trauma. But when I accompanied Cache to her session, I watched Dr. Leon uncomfortably stumble over words and be unable to speak directly about the attack; using euphemisms like "that thing that happened." When we got home, I called her and Cache never had to see her again.

Cache's Journal
January 12, 2001

> *I'm in school right now. I am not afraid of school but of what happened. I'm scared I won't be able to survive this. I just want it to disappear and never come back. But it won't and I hate it. I keep remembering all the time—his face, the police, the hospital and then when I went to see the ADA, I wish it had never happened, any of it, and I'd do anything to make it go away and never come back. I remember too much and I hate it I hate it I hate it. What did I do to deserve this?*

A therapist friend of my sister's recommended a woman therapist in the Village who specialized in post traumatic stress disorder, and over the next year Cache worked successfully with her toward resolving her fears.

twenty two

When all at once I saw a crowd,
A host of golden daffodils
William Wordsworth

While I had been busy with Julie's care and Cache's growing up, my vibrant and independent mother was evaporating.

She had spent her childhood living in back of a candy store with her single mother and brother, and grown into a vital, beautiful, dedicated young woman who graduated from law school before she was twenty-one, and went on to become an attorney. Each morning, when I was young, she took me to school before going into the city to her office. I remember her as a domineering tower of strength whom I first clashed with in my adolescence and then again and again throughout my life.

But now, that special, complex being had disappeared, leaving in her place a fragile shell. In recent years, my sister and I had noticed her aging, her slowed movement, and her reports of falling. I'd gotten her an alarm to wear around her neck after she refused to have someone come in to help her. She joked about the TV ad of a woman calling out "Help I've fallen and can't get up," each time I visited and reprimanded her when I found the device lying on a table far out of her reach.

On the morning I called and heard her slurred speech, my sister and I rushed out to the house. We found her in her bed, barely able to move. The last thing she remembered, she said, was falling down the circular staircase as she

121

was going up to bed the night before with a glass of water. She didn't remember how she had dragged herself back up the staircase and into bed.

We took her to the hospital where she was just being treated for some small cracked bones in her neck. After the first day her speech had cleared and wasn't slurred anymore, and there were no signs of the stroke she probably had had. But by the third day she began to disintegrate. When I came to visit, she told me they locked her in a closet at night; then she asked me where her husband was. When I told her he had died forty years ago, she very calmly said "Oh. No one told me." To make matters worse the psychiatric medications, the doctors then began to give her, made her even more out of touch with reality. As she progressively got more confused, they were unable to explain why or offer a solution. After a week, I knew I had to get her out of there and back to her beloved house.

My sister and I arranged for a nurse to stay with her and we each visited one day a week. Every time I came, I sat next to her on the couch and held her close, stroked her arm, and told her I loved her. She was so passive, so open and vulnerable I felt like I was the mother and she was the child. From not ever touching me as a child or saying she loved me, now she would sit there leaning into my arms, murmuring that she loved me too. Sometimes her eyes were vacant, and sometimes she looked focused, as if she had a secret life going on inside her wasted body.

After Julie's death, my mother continued to get weaker. Cache had always looked forward to her visits with Grandma, who had given her free range over her jewelry box and collection of silk scarves and high heel shoes, which she loved to prance around wearing. Now, Cache was sad to see her grandmother just sit on the couch, barely speaking and half asleep. She even missed the times Grandma yelled at her for making a mess. After a while she didn't want to come with me to visit because it made her feel too sad. I wished I had that choice.

At first, my sister and I had decided not to tell my mother when Julie died. But on one of my visits a few weeks later I thought she should know. When I told her she looked at me blankly and said "I'm sorry to hear that, I wish I could have met her." I felt a knife go through my heart. How could she not remember the love of her life? We were sitting on the couch and I didn't know what to say. I just began to hug her and caress her forehead. Images of my mother and Julie in the kitchen flashed through my mind. Julie on a step stool next to Grandma, who was showing her how to put the chocolate icing on the Duncan Hines white cake they had just taken from the oven. Then both of them licking the spatula as they rinsed out the mixing bowl in the sink. Years later, in our kitchen, my mother repeated her cake-icing lessons with Cache. I was afraid to ask her if she remembered Cache. At that moment, I didn't want to know.

I continued working for my sister and loving every minute of our being together. Then, one sunny morning, my sister called me into her office and tearfully asked me to accompany her to an oncologist. I knew she had been having increasingly painful back pain and had gone for tests over the past few weeks. The last I heard was that her doctor had not found any reason for the pain. But that day I took a cab with her to Fifth Avenue and Seventy-Sixth Street and sat next to her in the office of a classic doctor type with grey hair and mustache and steel-rimmed glasses. He told her in a cold, aloof voice that she had pancreatic cancer that could not be treated and that she had six months to live.

As we numbly sat in the cab after leaving his office, she took my hand and said:

"Oh, God, Leni, I'm so sorry to make you go through this all over again."

In the midst of this nightmare I felt my loss of Julie more strongly. With her gone and my mother fading, I couldn't bear the thought of losing my sister as well. To get through those days and long nights, I began my quest for a memorial to keep Julie's memory alive. I didn't want her to just disappear. First, I fantasized about having enough money for a children's hospital wing dedicated to her memory. Then I spoke with the people at the Institute where we learned the patterning techniques that helped prolong and enhance her life, about setting up a scholarship program for a needy child. They said they would try to figure out a way to implement the idea, but they never got back to me. When a friend of mine told me about someone dedicating a bench in Riverside Park for a loved one, I knew this was the perfect memorial for Julie.

Julie had always loved going to Riverside Park which is directly in back of our apartment building. I have scrapbook memories of Stu and me walking there, with her in her carriage, and then with her playing in the grass and on the swings. We had picnics and played ball there, and that was where she attempted to train her cat to walk on a leash. Later she learned to ride her bike there and walked her dog, Dorie. After she came home from the hospital, this was where her caretakers took her in her stroller for outings. Each time, when they returned, I heard about the people who had stopped to say hello to her. Some had known her before her illness, some were neighbors or patterners, and some had just been drawn to her in her stroller, watching the world with her wide, all-encompassing blue eyes. This was the perfect memorial for Julie and the timing was perfect.

The lower section of Riverside Park had just been renovated with new benches, walkways, and reseeded lawns, culminating at the Seventy-Second Street entrance, with the bronze half-seated statue of Eleanor Roosevelt guarding over it all. I chose a bench across from our building, within view of Eleanor, where I envisioned all who knew Julie might come to sit.

I felt it crucial that the creation of this memorial be shared by all who had known Julie: the patterners who were her extended family all these years, and the other friends who were part of our lives. I wrote notes to all I had addresses for and soon started receiving encouraging notes back, including checks. One evening Cache added seven dollars she had to the pile of checks, saying she wanted to be part of the collection. Soon there was enough for the bench, as well as enough extra to plant a tree on the big lawn across the pathway in front of where her bench would be. I picked a catalpa tree, which I was told was the only flowering tree that would thrive in that particular area of the park. It was still a young sapling when they planted it. Its thin, gangly limbs reminded me of Julie. Through the years the limbs have grown longer and the tree taller, but not much thicker. I watch each spring as the limbs fill with bright green leaves and hanging pods that then burst forth in a multitude of delicately scented white flowers for a few weeks in June.

We had a dedication ceremony in late summer of 2000. Lynette, Julie's caretaker, came with her husband, Franklin, and her two children, JJ and Tenesha, who had grown up knowing Julie. Franklin and JJ brought their steel-band instruments, and their vibrant sound filled the park that afternoon. Lynette finally had the chance, with Tenesha, to sing "Amazing Grace" and all four of them, in white flowing gowns, played and sang for Julie. Patterners and friends also spoke and recited poetry. My sister came, looking gaunt and weary from her latest round of chemo. Cache joined me in reciting a favorite poem of

Julie's from her younger days "I Wandered Lonely as a Cloud," which ends with "and my heart with pleasure fills, and dances with the daffodils."

When Julie died, Cache painted a picture of her floating on a cloud up in the sky. I often walk by her bench to say hello. I feel her presence there and by her tree much more than I do at her gravesite. Sometimes I sit for a while and imagine her up in heaven, floating on that cloud, freed at last from her stroller, my mother and sister by her side, with Julie in particular watching over Cache and me. The plaque on Julie's bench reads:

Julie Robin Goodman (1967-1998)
With love from those whose lives she touched
She.....dances with the daffodils

twenty three

I am not resigned to the shutting away of loving hearts in the hard ground

Edna St. Vincent Millay

September 11, 2001, the World Trade towers were collapsing, and my sister was dying of pancreatic cancer.

It was a bright and sunny morning, just before nine and I was on my way to my sister's law practice, where I had been working for almost two years. Cache had just started seventh grade at Stephen Gaynor. The skunk episode was fading into memory except for some isolated flashbacks. My sister wasn't in the office this week. She and several friends were on a ship approaching Rome and anticipated returning to the states in the next few days. The way she dealt with her illness was to plan a trip; feeling the act of making the next reservation assured her that she would be here to take that trip.

As I got on the Number 5 bus, the driver announced that the streets were closed off midtown because a plane had hit the World Trade Center. I imagined an accident similar to the 1945 crash of a small plane into the Empire State Building, and I went back to reading my newspaper. When I got off the bus at Fifty-Seventh Street and Broadway, I saw police everywhere, diverting traffic uptown. As I entered our office, I saw some of my fellow workers in tears. They were sitting around the secretary's desk listening to a small portable radio. The door to the office next door was open, with people gathered around a TV set on one of the desks. Between answering phone calls coming in canceling appointments I kept going back to the TV screen next door.

Then the second plane hit and it was clear that this was a terrorist attack. I watched as the first tower went down and the details of the third plane, heading toward Washington, DC, began to be broadcast. I started thinking about Cache in school and was thankful that she was uptown, far from harm.

My emotions were torn between the enormous tragedies enfolding in front of my eyes and the horror I had been living with since my sister had been diagnosed the previous summer. After being told by two oncologists that she had four to six months to live, she found a doctor at NYU Medical Center who was using a new drug protocol. He thought that if she could tolerate the drug, she might have more time.

Julie had died three years before, and our mother this past April. The image of Joan dying, with nothing that could be done to stop the course, seemed more than I could bear. Besides the nightmare of her getting worse and worse and in more and more pain, I was petrified that I would be the only one left for Cache, and when I died she would be utterly alone. I had just recently told Cache that Aunt Joan was sick, but not how sick. She had had so many losses, I wanted to shield her from this next one as long as possible.

As I watched the multiplying devastation that was unfolding in front of me on the TV, I started to worry about Cache, wondering what she had been told and how the school was handling this crisis. Finally, I called the school and was told by the secretary that they were in the midst of deciding how to present the events to the students. I offered our apartment to anyone who would not be able to get home, as we lived just three blocks away, and I asked her to make sure to tell Cache that I was OK.

I kept thinking about my sister on her way to Rome. It had been a year since her diagnosis and she was still alive. The experimental treatment had given her more time than we had ever believed. And because she was still alive and active, diminished in energy, but active, we had begun to believe that she would keep going forever. She kept working between chemotherapy treatments, although she was not strong enough to do the rigorous trial work. And she continued to travel every few months to far off exotic locales.

One client was due in our office for a deposition by his wife's attorney. The attorney had just cancelled, and I was trying to contact our client, to no avail. At eleven he appeared, completely distraught. He lived in Brooklyn and had been trying to call his children's housekeeper ever since he had emerged

128

from the subway downtown and heard what had happened. The police would not let him go back to Brooklyn, so he began making his way uptown on foot as subways were no longer running. We finally got through for him on our office phone. His housekeeper was hysterical, telling him of seeing from their window the planes hit and the buildings fall. Talking with him and helping him contact his children and then his estranged wife, intertwined with watching the drama relentlessly unfold on the TV screen, had thrust me into the unfolding drama, and I no longer felt like just another paralyzed viewer.

Then I got a hysterical call from Cache. Before the teachers could tell them about the plane crash, several parents appeared at school to take their children home and the story was circulating that we were at war. Cache was frantic that I might be hurt and couldn't get to her. I reassured her I was fine, that Fifty-Seventh Street was far away from the crash scene, and that I would be there as soon as I could get uptown. I was trying to tie up loose ends before I left the office, because I didn't know when I would be able to return. When I finally got outside, I realized there were no buses, and I joined the mass of people making their way on foot up Central Park West. Suddenly I found myself crying. All around me, people who didn't know each other were in intimate conversation with those walking alongside, trading information about where they started from and what they saw. Some people had portable radios on full blast, and I found myself gravitating toward them to hear the latest news and then pass it on to others. Tears were running down many other faces, and I felt intimately tied to every single person around me making that journey home. I had an urge to reach out and hug them all. As we continued walking uptown, we saw several buses filled to overflowing, inching up Central Park West along with cars also filled with people. When someone saw a bit of space they hailed the bus and were able to slip in among the throng. A few car drivers, having room for an additional passenger, yelled out their destinations and immediately had grateful takers.

Tears kept flowing down my cheeks as I made my way uptown. When I got to Seventy-Fourth Street, I said goodbye to my walking mates, wished them well, and crossed the avenue toward Cache's school. As I got closer to it I saw her on the steps, crying, as she looked up and down the street. I began waving and running toward her. Finally she saw me and ran down the steps toward my open arms. We hugged and hugged as she kept crying. We took an also tearful friend of hers, Nina, who lived in Queens, home with us, as a closed Queensboro Bridge barred her parents from coming to get her. The three of us, hugging and crying and comforting each other, walked back to our apartment and into the never-ending replay of the towers falling and people dying.

By the time my sister flew home two days later, the smell of the burning buildings and the soot had made their way uptown and into our every breath. When I saw her, it was clear she was fading. Over the next few weeks I trekked with her back and forth to the hospital, holding on to her tightly as she was losing her battle, while at night I numbly watched the TV screen as the rest of the world dealt with 9/11.

A few months before she died, my sister had attended a very elegant funeral at Temple Emanuel, a large prestigious institution at Fifth Avenue and Sixty-Fifth Street, and fantasized that her funereal might take place there. After her death, her law partner, Marcia, called in all of Joan's cards, and miraculously, the necessary strings were pulled. In order to have a service at Temple Emanuel one had to be a member of the congregation. Abracadabra, my sister was posthumously granted that honor and a noontime memorial service was arranged, to be held in the immense main synagogue auditorium.

I knew my sister was an important and well-loved attorney and founder of the New York State Women's Bar Association, and that her friends included many judges as well as attorneys, but I was not prepared for the enormous turnout. Some judges even suspended their morning sessions to attend Joan's funeral. The Chief Justice of New York State, Judith Kaye, was there. She was one of the speakers, along with Marcia, two other good friends, and of course me. Joan's three closest friends, along with me, Cache and Cache's best friend Nina, who had gotten permission to be off from school, were led into the rabbi's chamber. The rabbi pinned the black ribbons on us, made the razor cut, and asked me to make a deep tear in a scarf I brought. Then we were escorted into the now completely full auditorium, where my eyes caught sight of Joan's casket draped with an enormous wreath of white flowers positioned just in front of the podium. As we moved to sit in the first row, I saw a sea of faces through my now tearing eyes. Then I noticed, to the left, folding doors to an adjacent auditorium being rolled aside. It was in the midst of filling with more of my sister's mourners. Cache held my hand tightly, and with her other hand was clutching Nina's. I was the last speaker. When I walked to the podium to face that enormous sea of caring faces, I did not know that my opening words would have the devastating effect they did on Cache. As the events of the next few years played out, she blamed them on her feeling she was alone in the world and needed to find a way to survive without me. Those words were: "This is one time too many to be up here. When Julie died three years ago, my sister Joan was there with me. When Grandma died in April, my sister Joan was there with me. This time, when I look around for Joan, she's not there."

The woman rabbi did not know my sister but had listened to what Marcia and I had told her, and she delivered a caring and knowledgeable speech.

We sat Shiva at my house, with several close friends of Joan generously ordering the food each day. I had not called Terri, but she showed up at my apartment on Sunday afternoon saying she learned of Joan's death from an attorney friend of hers. We sat and talked for a while, bringing each other up to date on our lives. Her mother and father had both died since we last saw each other. As I sat there with her, I kept hearing a snippet of lyrics from *Chorus Line* echoing in my head: "I feel nothing. I feel nothing."

When Cache was eight years old, she wrote: "A family is a mother, a sister, an aunt and a grandmother." Cache's family was now down to two.

twenty four

I could not believe my sister, my little sister, was no longer a phone call away. Whenever I read something about a lawyer or a judge she knew, I wanted to call and tell her the news.

As much as I longed for my sister's presence, my immediate concern was how to help Cache process all these new losses. Her history was filled with losses—the first being given up by her mother, then having to leave Ommi and the others in her foster family, and now losing her sister, her grandmother and her aunt, I feared she would retreat into her depression again.

Cache's Journal: Monday May 6, 2002

The last few weeks I've just felt like crying and crying. Talking seems to annoy people, so I've just kept it inside of me. This pain inside of me just keeps growing and growing. And it's all mixed up with feeling and thinking that if my sister, Grandma, and especially my aunt hadn't died I wouldn't feel this way. Then I think if my sister Debora was living with me, I could just crawl up in her lap and tell her everything instead of writing all this down in a book. The other day I was looking at some pictures of my Mom when she was a baby and I felt kind of jealous, cause I don't and never will have any of me. Then I saw some pictures of my aunt and I wanted to call her and tell her, but then I remembered that she was dead.

At the end of this term, in June, Cache would be aging out of the Gaynor program. Now that she was in the seventh grade and entering puberty, I began to get reports from teachers of her being overly flirtatious with boys. They were concerned that she might have problems in the less monitored world of a junior high school setting, which she would be entering in the fall. I began to look for a school where she would receive the same kind of emotional and academic support she had flourished with in Gaynor. I visited several and narrowed the field down to three. Cache strongly wanted to go to York Prep because two of her good friends were also going there. I tossed a coin in my head and accepted her choice.

Cache had completed her PTS therapy and stopped thinking about Skunk most of the time. I thought this would be a good time to connect her with a new therapist to help deal with her new losses and with this big change from the protected environment at Gaynor to the potentially problematic new freedoms she would encounter as a teen. I found a new therapist, Jeanette, who worked specifically with problem teens. Cache liked her immediately and I breathed a sigh of relief.

Cache's Journal September 3, 2002 12:36am

I start school on the 12th which is next Thursday. Honestly, I'm so scared. I mean this is a whole new school and a bunch of kids I don't even know. In some ways I wish I could be 12 forever. I'm really scared not to be going into Mr. O'Hare's classroom and having him teach me. Stephen Gaynor is where I learned everything I know, literally. I learned how to work hard, how to solve math problems, understand history. And most importantly how to take responsibility for what I've done and face reality. I'm scared to death to let others teach me.

Cache began York Prep in September 2002. For the first time, she was able to go out for lunch, which meant she could socialize with the pubescent boys who had all of a sudden entered her life. Almost immediately, she became involved with some rebels who snuck away at lunchtime and smoked cigarettes, which one boy's older sister got for him. Cache who had begged her aunt to stop smoking, was now smoking and helping seventh graders obtain cigarettes from this boy as well. She also became attracted to a boy in her class, Bryan, who had a history of drug abuse. Within a month, she was sneaking out of school with him, and during school they were often found in the locker room making out. This escalated to her not coming home after school or sneaking away to meet him after she came home. At first the school called only me, until I insisted they also call Bryan's mother after each incident when they were found in the locker room or upper hallway.

Cache's Journal Friday October 18, 2002

I'm alone again. I'm doing so badly in school. I'm failing science and I'm about to fail Spanish, not that I care. I hate my teacher. But the thing is that my Mom is really disappointed. She's not saying it but I can see it in her eyes and I never wanted to let her down. Also someone starts a rumor that I met Bryan in the locker room downstairs and somehow it got to the teachers and they told my Mom.

As the weeks and months went on, Cache continued her defiant behavior. I was now driving her to school each morning, but as soon as I left she would sneak out of the building. The school began to require her to stay in the lunchroom instead of going out with the other students, only to have her sneak out behind a monitor's back. One day a teacher intercepted a note Cache had been exchanging with another student about her plans to meet Bryan in the unisex bathroom of Starbucks to have sex, with her friend cautioning her to make sure she had him use a double condom. It was now clear that whatever restrictions the school asked her, and now him, to abide by, or whatever restrictions I imposed at home, nothing was working. And my thirteen year old daughter was slipping further and further away from me.

Jeanette, who was seeing Cache for depression, also now was needing to address Cache's behavior problems. As she saw what she called a "child at risk" behavior increasing, she finally advised me to explore sending her to a Wilderness Program, geared toward helping such young teens get back on the right track.

That last Friday afternoon, she was already running down the steps crying, when I got to her school. She walked quickly past me, saying "I don't want to talk. I just want to go home now." I tried to catch up with her but she kept moving faster each time I called to her to wait for me. By the time I was half way home, I had lost track of her. A familiar fear began to fill my gut that when I got home she would not be there, and I would not know where she was for hours and hours, as had happened so many times before.

But this time she was there. Her backpack, jean jacket, and shoes were strewn by the front door and she was lying on the couch curled up in a fetal position under her comforter. She looked pale and completely exhausted. When she felt me sit down next to her, she whispered "I hate my school and I never wanted to go back. I was caught with Bryan again, kissing at the lockers, and I'm not going to sign that stupid contract the Dean wants me to. I'm not going to promise to go to study hall and do my homework, and not sneak out of class to meet Bryan, and all the other stupid things they want me to do."

I put my hand on her shoulder and tried to comfort her. "You don't have to go back to school. This is the time for you to go to the Wilderness Program that Jeanette talked to us about, where you'll be in a safe place, with therapy and support every day." She turned away from me, still entwined in her comforter, shutting me out of any further discussion. I left her there and went to the computer to retrieve the application papers for the program; and to think through how to engineer the next step as Cache appeared too traumatized to participate in any decision-making.

When I returned to the living room she was gone. I called several of her friends, who usually knew where she was—but they had not heard from her. Nor had Bryan's mother.

At 9:15pm, I still hadn't heard from her. Finally at 11:30pm, Cache angrily stormed in and into her bedroom, slamming the door behind her. In the middle of the night, I heard her move into the living room and turn on the TV. She stayed on the couch most of the weekend, except for when I took her to talk with Jeanette on Saturday afternoon. In a tearful and very subdued session, she agreed she was ready to go to the wilderness program. When we got home, she went back to the couch and curled up with her comforter again. BB, her fuzzy little white dog, checked in on me once in a while during the rest of the weekend, but mostly stayed posted next to Cache on the couch.

Cache's Journal April 15, 2003

I saw Jeanette today and finally agreed to go to some wilderness program later this week. Before I agreed I made my Mom and Jeanette promise I could see my friends and Bryan before I go. They both agreed, although my Mom didn't look thrilled about it. I guess after yesterday she wouldn't be. She probably thinks if I see my friends again before she sends me away I'll make some plan to run away again with Bryan. But I'm not going to. I just want to be with my friends before I go away for a month. I know a month doesn't sound like much, but to me it seems like forever. I feel like my life might as well be over. I can't imagine not being able to see Bryan for a whole month. You might as well tell me not to breathe for a whole month. I just want to go and get it over with so I can come back. God I feel so drained. All I want to do is sleep and watch TV so I can zone the fuck out and forget that everything is falling apart around me—everything except him—he's my light at the end of the tunnel.

I decided not to tell her exactly when she was going to the program, as I was worried she'd panic and run away again. In the weeks leading up to this decision I had envisioned asking Stu, my ex-husband and now Cache's godfather, to accompany us to Boise, Idaho. But after Friday's episode, I worried that Cache would try to run away sometime during the trip—on the way to the airport, or when we changed planes in Salt Lake City. All of a sudden, the once unthinkable choice seemed the only possible one. I contacted the escort service the Wilderness Program director had recommended. On Sunday morning, in a few hours of faxing back and forth, the plan was set in motion. All I had to do was make plane reservations for the two escorts to come to New York, and for the flight to Idaho.

Cache never questioned whom I was calling or faxing all weekend. It was as if she knew what was happening and was leaving it in my hands. She looked so fragile and sad. I sat with her at times and attempted to comfort her with my words and touch. She allowed me to rub her head and back and talk to her.

"We can't do this ourselves anymore. I'm going to send you to a place that will help you. You need to be brave and everything will be all right again."

The two escorts, Marcia and Robert, would arrive at 4am the next morning. During the day, I tiptoed around, packing a bag with Cache's contact lenses, glasses, vitamins, medications, and underwear. Everything else would be given to her at the program. All I had to do was wake up Cache when they got here, introduce them, and tell her she would be safe with them taking her to the program. Then I was supposed to leave the apartment. "No way," I said. "I'll go into the bedroom, but I will not leave the apartment."

Early Sunday evening I suggested to Cache that she take a leisurely bath, wash her hair, shave her legs, and give herself a manicure. She agreed so quickly that I was sure she knew she would be leaving in the morning. She stayed on the couch again that evening in her favorite black velour sweat pants and top with her big comforter wrapped around her. BB, restlessly moved back and forth from the living room couch to my bed all through the night.

I couldn't sleep at all, even getting the flashing lights before my eyes that I had once before, right after Julie died. Cache was watching TV on the couch in the living room as I tiptoed to the hall closet and found the nose spray to open my tightened blood vessels a doctor had given me at that time. Then I made my way back to my bedroom with flashing lights in my eyes and the spray in my hand, to wait.

My cell phone, under the pillow, rang at 4am. Marcia and Robert were outside our building. I tiptoed into the kitchen and called down to the doorman for him to send my two guests up without calling me when they arrived. Cache was sound asleep on the couch. My heart was pounding and I was having trouble getting my breath as I stood and watched her from our long hallway, lined with our family pictures, waiting for them to reach our unlocked front door.

I tried to get a feeling of who these strangers were, as we I stood in the dining area about to sign documents, giving them permission to transport my daughter across state lines. Marcia was a friendly, matronly-looking midwestern type woman in her mid forties. Her husband worked at SUWS, the Wilderness Program, and she assured me she had a lot of positive experience escorting teens to the program. Robert, tall and slightly gray-haired, also seemed friendly and assured me I did not have to worry. He had flown in from Boston to be the driver and escort for Marcia and Cache to La Guardia. If all went well, he then would hop a plane back to Boston. Otherwise, he would continue on with them to Idaho. I took a gigantic breath and signed the papers. I also gave Robert the bag I had packed for Cache, Then, as if walking in a dream, I went to the couch and sat down next to my daughter. I touched her arm, which all of a sudden seemed so tiny and frail, and gently woke her. Still half asleep, she looked over my shoulder at the two figures. Like a robot, I introduced them and told her they would be taking her to the Wilderness Program and that I thought this was the best way for her to go. I leaned in to kiss her but she pushed me away. I made myself stand up, said "goodbye my darling," then made myself walk into my bedroom and close the door. Immediately, I leaned into the door edge as close as I could to hear how she was reacting. I couldn't hear clearly so I opened the door a crack. Cache sounded calm and compliant. She was in her bedroom with Marcia and I heard her ask if she could pack a few things. Marcia told her she would get everything she needed there. Then I heard the apartment door close. I ran to the living room windows. Soon I saw two outlines walking very close to each and then calmly getting into the back seat of a car. Then a taller figure got into the drivers seat and the car drove away.

After it was out of sight, I slowly walked down the hallway into Cache's room. I sat down on the edge of her bed and stared at the Eminem poster on the wall above her shiny white dresser. As I stared at him looming over her room, I saw in his image all her anger and defiance this past year–his open sweat shirt, his tattooed navel, and his jockey underpants exposed above his low hanging sweat pants. I looked at his sullen, piercing eyes under the rag doo tied around his head. I felt anger toward him, and at all the rap music that filled my daughter's head. I wanted to tear him off her wall and stomp on him and smash all the CDs with the forbidden lyrics that friends had burned for her. I wanted to throw her spiked bracelets and tight belly shirts down the incinerator–as though that would change things and bring my sweet little girl back to me. Instead I lay back on her pillow, buried my face into her pile of stuffed animals, and cried. BB jumped onto the bed next to me and nuzzled his warm nose in under my elbow. I began to feel all the tension of the last year seep out of my body….and I finally could let go of that runaway locomotive I had been trying to hold back but had instead been dragged by it down the track, unable to even slow it down a bit.

twenty five

Hope is a thing with feathers
That perches in the soul
Emily Dickenson

Without Cache the house felt empty. I was alone for the first time in my life, except for two months between roommates when I was in my twenties. I was alone in my apartment. The home I created for my children and myself. Alone, except for BB, my daughter's dog, now my companion. He wandered through the house looking for Cache, as I did at times.

I had gone from living at home, to living in the city with roommates, to living with Stu. Even when we divorced I was not alone because Julie was with me. The next decade was filled with Julie and caretakers and volunteers. Then Terri was with me for ten years, and when we broke up, Julie was still with me. Then Cache arrived and was with me even after Julie died. Now that I had sent Cache away to the Idaho Mountains to learn how to take care of herself, I was finally alone and it was time for me to learn how to take care of myself.

I received my first letter from Cache about a week after she left.

Dear Mom:

I am writing to you for a couple of reasons. First off I want to let you know that I am extremely mad at you for sending me here on Monday and not telling me. I think that was really shitty.

Next I'd like to say that I'm not crazy about SUWS, but I will admit that it is OK and I've learned some good things. But it is always really cold in the morning and then extremely hot while we are hiking. And a lot of the time we walk about 5 miles a day and then have to sleep on the ground. We always have oatmeal for breakfast and pitas with peanut butter and apricots for lunch. Then for dinner we switch on and off with rice and lentils, bad chili Mac or extremely bad burritos. We also have to drink 4-5 bottles of water everyday. Our instructors are Susie and Doug. Susie is pretty cool but I don't like Doug. He's sorta mean and strange.

As for the kids, I can't find a word to describe them. Sierra, from Texas, is here because she was raped by her father when she was little and now he abuses her. Also she had some eating disorders. Then there is Brigit, who is from Queens, I think she is here because at times she has a lot of anger. Cynthia says she's from Turkey, but also claims to live in three different states. No one believes her. She is here because she is on probation for using a weapon on three boys. She also was raped and abused by her father and has anger management problems. Both she and Brigit are Goths. Cynthia believes and worships the devil. Then there is Katrina from Oregon. She has a drinking problem and has had sex with a lot of different guys. None of the girls are virgins and think it is strange that I am one and they think of me as lower than them.

Sierra, Brigit and Cynthia are violent at times. It's kind of scary. A few days ago, Brigit and Sierra beat each other up while we were hiking. Cynthia keeps running away and Kat has just been taken away somewhere. Last night Cynthia started going insane and saying a demon was coming to get her. She plopped down next to Kat on my bed screaming and going nuts and I was scared shitless. I tried to stay calm. Then out of nowhere Brigit slapped Kat...and then they started going at each other. Right now it is really late at night. My hand is getting cramped and I have to go and eat.

The main point of writing this to you is to let you know that I do not feel safe here at all and want to come home. I feel like I have accomplished all I could and can. I am ready to face the world again. I even feel like I have more self esteem and can take care of myself and know what's wrong and right and how to choose. So please let me come home. Please, I love you and just want to come home.
Love Cache

I started to pick up the phone to call the staff and ask for her to be placed in a safer group. Then I stopped myself from running to her rescue. I had before me the letter from the program forewarning parents about our child's first few letters home. It listed the most common triggers our desperate offspring would reach for to shock us into taking them home. Cache instinctively knew what I would respond to: bad food, unhealthful living conditions, and unsafe companions. I was touched that she did recognize her need to be there and that she did not make up stories about being abused by the staff or molested by all the lesbians, which were also listed as possible triggers our daughters might use as rescue ammunition.

The next step in the program was for me to send Cache an impact letter telling her all the reasons I sent her to SUWS, and which she would have to read to the rest of her group in family circle around the campfire.

Over the weeks, her letters changed slowly from begging to come home to understanding more about herself and gaining new strengths. After resisting the rules and confines of the program for the first two weeks, she settled into activities that were meant to build upon her strengths and give her confidence in her ability to change and make progress.

Dear Mom:

I know you don't believe me, but I am now honestly able to make the right choices. So please let me come home before April 28th cause I want to be home for Julie's anniversary. I don't want to light the candle here. I don't think you understand how much I need to be home for that date.

I'm not leaving in the middle, because I have already done what I needed to do and what you wanted me to do. And I don't think it is fair for you to send me to boarding school before you see if I've changed for the better and don't need to go to boarding school at all. Please don't send me to boarding school before September. Please give me a chance to prove myself.
I love you lots, Cache

She slowly progressed through the six levels of the program, from Mouse to Eagle, backtracking each time she met a difficult challenge, regrouping with the help of the staff and her fellow mates to meet the obstacle. Each time she conquered the prescribed tasks and moved up to the next phase, I read the program's objectives and tried to visualize her growth:

Phase 1. (Mouse): Personal responsibility–ability to recognize and maintain basic self care and well being; making shelters and backpacks.

Phase 2 (Raccoon): Respect and Cooperation–awareness and respect for the needs of others; caring for the llamas who carried their supplies; making deadfall traps; and basic fire making skills with flint and steel.

Phase 3 (Frog): Determination–Acquiring confidence by successfully completing bow drill technique of fire making; improving previous skills.

Phase 4 (Buffalo): Patience–better communication and working with others; learning patience and determination thru bow drill mastery; cooking food for group.

Phase 5 (Wolf): Trust–in one's own ability to deal with situations that arise; learning to trust others; gaining ability to express concerns and help each other; ropes challenge course and solo experience.

Phase 6 (Eagle): Vision of Future and Service–owning success and mastery of new skills and perspectives; how to use them after leaving SUWS.

I spoke with Cache's therapist, Jon, each week. He told me she was learning to persevere and make progress in many areas. But she closed off emotionally and was oppositional whenever she was required to reveal herself or felt vulnerable. She did excel in any task where she could help another student and which would take the pressure off her to perform.

I continued to receive letters begging me to take her home, but I was warned by the program staff and by her therapist that these six weeks were not enough time to make the changes she needed to function safely in the world. They recommended that she needed to continue her growth in a therapeutic residential setting. Her discharge report also stated a need for further evaluation of potential attachment issues, which at that time I did not truly understand.

She did not take this news well.

Dear Mom:

Jon had just told me that I'm going to be staying here until I am done with all the levels. He also told me that it sounds like I will then be going to a boarding school right away. So I don't get the point why you even sent me here to make me get better if you're not going to bother to see if I have changed. I am so sick of your bullshit. You are so cruel and unfeeling that I don't even know how I could be your kid. I swear to god and on my life I will never at all in my life forgive you for this. And you have now lost your chance to see the new me. I hope you rot in hell.

I sat at my desk immobilized by the anger that had just spewed forth from my fax machine. I felt helpless because I couldn't make her better. I wanted to hold her in my arms and kiss all the bad and pain away. But I kept reminding myself, while trying to ignore the pain deep inside my chest that had been there since I sent her away, that Cache had to do this herself.

As Cache was beginning her journey, I had a journey I needed to take as well, and so I went back into therapy. I had always turned to therapy in times of crisis or change. When Stu and I were beginning to fall apart, we went to couples therapy, and when that therapist calmly told us our marriage was doomed, I went to individual therapy to work through my sadness and "move on." When Julie was diagnosed with her brain tumor and given six months to live, I went to primal scream therapy to scream my pain and sadness away. I screamed and screamed each week for over a year and was always amazed that there was more screaming left. Therapy helped me leave acting and begin a new career in counseling after Julie came home from the hospital. Years later, Terri and I turned to therapy to try to hold onto our relationship. It kept us patched up for several years, and then I finally turned to individual therapy again to help me understand what went wrong and to move on without her. Now I was turning to therapy again, this time to help me figure out who I was without a partner, without my work life, and now apart from my child.

Cache had been in Wilderness for six weeks when I flew to Boise, Idaho. There I rented a car and drove north two hours to a campsite to be with her when she received her graduation certificate for "completing with honors the rigorous course of learning and personal development of the SUWS Youth Program." I, who had never camped out in my life and never wanted to, was on my way to spend twenty-four hours with my daughter in a tent in the middle of the Idaho Rockies.

When I arrived at the desert-like patch of land that was their campsite, Cache was nowhere to be seen. I met two other mothers who were being greeted with hugs and kisses from their kids, but Cache remained back at her tent, ignoring me. I stayed in the main tent talking with her counselors for about an hour. Finally, Sierra, the other girl who was graduating, went back to her tent and dragged Cache out to meet me. She was wearing a light gray sweat shirt and very baggy khaki cargo pants that folded over the top of muddy, high-top laced hiking boots. Her hair looked much longer than I remembered and she had it tied back into two braided pigtails. As she got closer, I saw how tanned she was and that my 5'2", 110-pound daughter looked even tinier than I remembered. I reached out to hug her but she just grunted a hello and walked ahead of me into the main tent. Trying to convey my love, I gently began with, "It's so good to see you." She shrugged, avoiding my eyes. Steeling myself for a further rebuke, I continued, "I know you're angry at me, but now that I'm here, can we try to talk? "She shrugged again, still not looking at me, and mumbled "OK". The knot inside my stomach relaxed a bit as I saw she was at least open to communicate.

Slowly, over the rest of the day, she accepted my presence, and I could feel her letting down her barriers as she showed me around the campsite and her tent. I heard pride in her voice as she explained she was going to be responsible for all our food and shelter. I felt we were reconnecting, and by nightfall her anger had faded away. She even allowed me to talk about the prospect of her going on to the next step in her recovery. We lay awake for hours, cuddled next to each other in our sleeping bags near the dying fire, which she had somehow started with a flint and a piece of wood. We talked about what we both had done during this time apart. Finally, listening to some animal howling in the distance, I fell asleep.

The next morning we were driven back to the base camp, where Cache and Sierra and David, who was also graduating, gleefully ran toward the shower rooms to wash the last few weeks of mud and dirt from their bodies. While Cache was washing her hair in the stall next to me, I took a quick shower and tried to stretch out my sore back muscles. I hoped I never had to spend another night in a tent. When she came out of the back room dressed in the new jeans and tee shirt I brought for her graduation ceremony, she was beaming. We all sat down with the staff for a breakfast of eggs and toast. Cache and I were next to her therapist, Jon, along with the other two graduates and their mothers and the counselors.

As the staff cleared the table and began to set up for the graduation ceremony, I took a deep breath and began to explain to Cache that Marcia was on her way over to escort her to Copper Canyon Academy, the therapeutic boarding school I had chosen near Sedona, Arizona. She started to cry.

"Cache, please try to be brave. You've done so well here. I want you to come home as much as you do, but you need to do this next step first."

"Mommy I love you so much. I just want to come home."

I took her in my arms and hugged her, not wanting to ever let go. I wanted to cancel Marcia and Copper Canyon and take my daughter home with me. Instead I forced myself to say, "My darling, my brave darling, it's really important that you take this next step, and then you will be able to come home."

"If I do good and show you I can take care of myself, can I come home after the summer?"

"Let's see how things go. We'll write and talk and I'll come to see you as soon as I am allowed."

"I promise I'm going to show you I can take care of myself. I promise."

The graduation ceremony started. It was very short, with the counselors and Jon praising the three graduates for completing all the steps in the rigorous wilderness program, hoping they would take with them what they learned and wishing them success in the future. Then they handed each graduate their certificate.

After we said our goodbyes, I walked outside with Cache and saw Marcia waiting in the parking lot. We hugged, with neither of us wanting to let go. I made myself kiss her goodbye and stood there waving as Marcia drove away with her to catch their plane to Phoenix. I held back my tears and all my doubts that I was doing the right thing. Then I drove back to the Boise airport with David and his mother, whom she was taking to a school in Washington. I kept wishing I had felt able to trust Cache enough to take her to her new school myself, and that she was sitting next to me in the car.

I boarded my plane and flew home alone as Marcia was handing Cache over to the Copper Canyon Academy intake team in the Phoenix airport. Like a mantra, I kept repeating to myself, "Cache is safe now, in a safe place with people who are trained to care for troubled teens."

twenty six

Copper Canyon Academy was a therapeutic residential school for teens thirteen to eighteen. I was told Cache would have an easier time acclimating to their strict behavior modification program because she had already gone through the rigorous six-week wilderness program. We would not be allowed any contact with each other, except by letter, for the first month or two, until she demonstrated her acceptance of being there and was working the program.

Friday May 9, 2003
Dear Cache:

I got home last night about midnight and I spoke with Marcia this morning about your trip to Phoenix. She said you were very quiet during the flight but seemed to listen to her about this being a chance for a new beginning.

It was very precious and also emotional for me to spend that time with you at wilderness. I was very impressed with the work you accomplished at SUWS and with your new skills, both physically and in your ability to take care of yourself. I think you are on the right path to help you the rest of your life. I am also in the process of making changes in the way I see you and react with you, and hopefully this will continue to improve our relationship

It is hard for me to be separated from you after spending those few days together, but I keep reminding myself this is the next step in your growth and in our growth as a family. I'm going to call Daddy and tell him how you conquered the great outdoors. I'll also call Debora and Michael and let them know what's going on and where you are. I would love to hear how your room is and who your roommates are and all the other stuff about the school.

It was so great to see you after you washed the desert off your body. Seeing you again was the best Mother's Day gift that I could ever have. Let me know what else you need from home. I love you with all my heart. P.S Your bed supplies should arrive today by UPS.

Cache's Journal entry May 8, 2003

Today is my first day here at Copper Canyon. They gave me a big sister. Her name is Jess. She's pretty cool. She explained to me all the rules and what I have to do to get out of level one. I'm OK but I really feel like I don't belong here—like I'm in the wrong place. I feel very lonely even though there are a whole bunch of girls around most of the time. Anytime I think of the future I feel like crying and curling up in a ball.

I wrote again even though I hadn't gotten a response from Cache.

Thursday May 15, 2003
Dear Cache:
    I think about you everyday and try to imagine what you are going through having to adjust to a new place again. Just keep remembering how lonely you felt when you first got to SUWS and then how it got better.
    I will be able to talk with your therapist each week and also your teacher and Ruth, the parent coordinator. So I will get some idea what is happening/. But I won't really know what you are thinking and feeling until you write to me. I hope you will write even though you are angry about not being able to come home. I'm going to take BB for a haircut tomorrow. His hair is so long I can't see his eyes. Daddy is coming over later today with a birthday present for me to send you. You are allowed to write to him also.
    I will write again soon and send your pictures from SUWS as soon as I get them back. I love love you.
Mommy

I was kept up to date on Cache's activities and progress, or rather lack of progress, by weekly phone calls with her therapist. As in the wilderness program, she resisted complying with the regulations and activities until it sank in there was no way she could win unless she played by the rules. At first she was so resistant she was moved back to Level Zero, and then even on "run risk,"

meaning she had to sleep on the living room couch and be shadowed during the day by a staff member because they found some money under her mattress, along with a necklace and a pair of earrings she had somehow hidden from all her body checks there and in wilderness.

May 21 2003
Dear Cache:

I just got the boxes from SUWS with your muddy, smelly clothing and things—you would not believe how bad it smelled when I opened them. BB came into your room to see what the smell was. I washed everything two or three times till the water ran clear—your boots still smell—hopefully a week on the windowsill will help.

I hung your bow drill on a hook on your bookcase. I am getting a package together to send you for your birthday. Let me know if there is anything you want from home. I thought I'd send your Curious George monkey and your stuffed panda. OK? Your teacher said you're ready to start 9th Grade English, Science and Art—That's great. I think it's a good idea she is continuing you in pre-Algebra and Spanish 1—Should I send your Spanish workbook? I love love you even though you don't think so at times. Please write to me.
Mommy

When I got my first letter, I felt my heart jumping as I tore open the envelope.

May 22
Dear Mom:

I finally was allowed to go back to my room and sleep in my bed again. You probably know I was put on run risk. This place is fucked up—all I did was refuse to give Ruth my special good luck necklace and favorite earrings—and the money they found under my mattress was just some change to call Bryan when I got to a phone. I don't know how anyone in their right mind would think it was enough to run away with. I can't wait to get the pictures from SUWS. I miss the other girls so much and also my therapist Jon. Could you also send me my pillow? The one they gave me is so flat I can't get comfortable on it. Also:
my 2 black tee shirts
some ankle socks and my stuffed animals

the new Harry Potter book and if there is a new "Daughters of the Moon"
the picture of me and my friends on my dresser
Even though I really don't think I need to be here, I will try to do all the steps I
need to move back up to Level One. Please send my love to Daddy and Debora
and Michael and give BB a big hug from me.
Love Cache

May 26
Dear Cache:

I just got your first letter. Thank you for writing. I will get a box together
and send, but so far I can't find one big enough for the pillow. Maybe the school
can lend you another one till I can send it. I had to go over your list with Ruth,
the parent coordinator. She told me I can't send any pictures of friends, even the
friends you made at SUWS. I can send pictures of you and the staff only—and
I can't send any clothing that is black. I made an album of the kids from
SUWS that I am saving for you on your desk.

You sound a little more at peace with yourself and where you are. I hope
you are truly starting to feel this way. I was very upset when you told me at
SUWS to go out and adopt another child and give up on you. The only reason
I sent you to SUWS and now to Copper Canyon is precisely because I am
never going to give up on you and move on to another child. I don't want another
child. You are my child and I will stick by you through this whole process and
know you will come out in the end a better adjusted and stronger person, able to
make healthy choices for yourself in your life ahead. I am also reading the Four
Agreements and would be interested in your analysis of how it can apply to your
own life. I am trying to work on that assignment myself now. I'll pass on your
hellos to your friends and send your love to Daddy and Debora and Michael.
Love, Mom

Cache's Journal entry June 4, 2003

Today is my birthday. I always wanted to turn 14, but now I don't. I wish
there was a way for me to stop the sun from setting and the moon from
rising. I can't believe I'm going to be spending my birthday here, with a
whole bunch of people I don't know and don't really care about and who

don't care about me. This morning I had to get up for a work hour and this afternoon when I reminded Jean that my birthday presents were downstairs she said each time I ask is one more day I won't get them. After that I went to the bathroom and cried. I thought about what could have been, the birthday party I should have had and the people who would have been there, and I thought about Bryan and also about the final exam I should have taken. This is the worst birthday I've ever had.

It took four months for her to give up her resistance and begin to move forward in the program. At this point we were allowed to communicate by letter and speak weekly, with her therapist on the phone, too.

In addition to the very rigorous behavior mod approach, the program was centered on The Four Agreements concept in the book by Miguel Ruiz. As I read the book and began to understand what Cache was experiencing, I too began to see changes I needed to make in my mothering and also in my life. The Four Agreements became a way of life for both of us.

The Agreements were:

Be Impeccable with Your Word

Don't Take Anything Personally

Don't Make Assumptions

Always Do Your Best

Finally, in her fifth month Cache moved back up to Level One, and then two months later on to Level Two, which allowed me to come for a two-day visit. In the meantime, I was noticing subtle changes in myself.

In the middle of July, after Cache had been away for almost four months, I woke up one morning relaxed, without butterflies in my stomach and that familiar feeling of angst. I hadn't felt this way for a long, long time, probably not since the early days with Terri next to me. I kept going to therapy, where week after week, I heard myself talking about Cache and her progress, even though I knew I needed to focus on me and what I wanted to do with my life, with no career or job to fill my days. Aside from therapy, my only commitments were walking BB and continuing my exercise routine most mornings. I looked around for activities that had sparked my interest in the past. I opened my grandmother's sewing machine, ready to begin a sewing project. I met friends for lunch, went to an afternoon movie or a new museum exhibition, and some days just curled up on the couch and read for a few hours, with nothing and no one to interrupt me. I began walking down to the pier along the Hudson River, now renovated and enhanced, courtesy of Donald Trump– in return for allowing him to construct massive, tall buildings that now blocked the waterside view. One afternoon I brought a notebook with me, and while I sat on one of the new benches overlooking the river, I began to write again after many years.

On the pier, I saw a sign about free weekend kayaking on the Hudson. The last time I was in a kayak was at a Club Med with Cache, when she was seven years old. The next Sunday, I excitedly walked down to the dock at Seventieth Street, signed a waiver, picked out a life preserver in my size, and got on line to wait for my turn. When the volunteer motioned me down the ramp and started to turn a kayak around for me to step into, I felt my stomach doing flip flops. I put on a big smile as I assured him I was a good swimmer and experienced kayaker. He helped me into the swaying kayak and pointed out the area I had to stay within during my allotted twenty minutes on the river. I kept smiling and nodding as I tried to remember how to hold the paddle and how to maneuver it through the water. He gave me a push off from the dock, and I was on my way. Once I got myself into a rhythm, I felt exhilarated as I made my first sweep up to the beginning of the Seventy-Ninth Street boat basin, then deftly turned my boat around and headed down toward the Sixty-Sixth Street pier area, and then back up again. By this time my shorts and sneakers were soaking wet from the water that somehow splashed or leaked into my kayak, and my palms were getting red from grasping the paddle. As I paddled back and forth, waving to others in their kayaks, seeing the George Washington Bridge in the distance and looking over at the buildings along Riverside Drive, I realized I was having fun. I even felt a bit high. My heart was filled with love for my rediscovered waterfront and my city and I began to cry. I was kayaking on the Hudson River. Who would have believed that possible a few years ago?

Then one weekend, for the first time in my life, I drove upstate and treated myself to a spa vacation. During my three days there, I pampered myself daily with a different treatment-a facial, a massage, a manicure and pedicure–and spent the remaining part of each day trying different meditating methods, taking yoga and exercise classes, eating delicious healthful food, meeting interesting people doing the same things, not needing to tell my story if I didn't want to. I couldn't remember how long it had been since I had no worries about what might be awaiting me at home and no immediate problems that I needed to solve.

twenty seven

On Thanksgiving Day I went to the movies. I thought I'd be the only one in the theatre, judging from the overflowing carts of my fellow shoppers in Fairway the day before, as I carried my basket with the half turkey breast, sweet potato, and small apple pie to the register. But when I got to the movie theatre it was full of people.

In the past, I would have been one of those with an overflowing cart, shopping and cooking for the big Thanksgiving gathering. First, all those years for my mother and sister and husband and Julie, then with Terri, and now more recently for Cache and close friends. But this year, those close friends, Joan and Di, were on another continent, and Cache was in a school in Arizona. I had been invited to share Thanksgiving with another friend and her family, but as the day grew closer I felt content within myself and didn't feel the need to break bread with someone else's family and friends.

My real Thanksgiving had been two weeks before, when I was finally allowed to visit Cache. At her request, I brought her an extra crispy chicken sandwich with potato wedges and root beer from KFC, and added a Fudge Brownie Earthquake Sundae from Dairy Queen. These two fast food havens were right across the road from each other at the Camp Verde exit off of highway I-17, high in the mountains, an hour's drive north from the Phoenix Airport. At that same junction was a Comfort Inn, a Burger King, a McDonald's, and a Denny's. I checked in at the Comfort Inn, picked up her food, and, directions in hand, began to make my way to her school, which was a few miles down a dusty road in the midst of the Yavapai-Apache Nation tribal land, deep in the desert-like Verde Valley. It was hard to believe that only fifteen minutes away were the magnificent red hills of Sedona.

I checked my hand-scribbled directions when the barren roadside gradually changed into a main street with one-story storefronts on either side. As I drove, I started getting butterflies in my stomach. I hadn't seen Cache for seven months. Aside from biweekly phone calls with her therapist on the line with us, we had only our letters to keep our connection alive. After a few blocks, I saw a gas station ahead and the fork where I needed to turn right, drive past the junk yard, and turn right again into the second side road, then make a sharp turn up a hill and into the parking lot of Cache's unmarked schoolyard. As I parked the car and bent over to gather my treasure trove of fast foods Cache had been craving all these months, I heard, "Mommy. Mommy, I've been waiting for you."

I looked up and saw my beautiful daughter, still very tanned, her shiny black hair now just past shoulder length, wearing khaki shorts, sneakers, and a blue tee shirt denoting her second-level status in the program, running toward me. I dropped the packages on the seat and welcomed her into my arms. She kept hugging and kissing me and we both started to cry. Then she helped me gather her goodies and we walked, arm in arm, from the small parking area, which appeared to double as a back yard, toward the cabin she shared with the other girls in the program.

As she gobbled down her KFC treat, I had a chance to meet the two house staff supervisors and a few of the other girls who were in the family room, some doing homework and others working on a jigsaw puzzle. The girls all wore khaki shorts with tee shirts in red, blue, maroon or green, depending on their level. Cache had been placed in this smaller of the two campuses where the younger students usually began. Most of the other girls were around her age. None of the girls I met were from New York, nor had they ever been there. One girl was from New Hampshire, and the others were from the midwest or west coast. They were all friendly and very polite and looked like normal teenagers, although I knew each one was there for a very serious reason. Cache's last letter to me talked about how fascinated everyone was that she was from New York, and they wanted to know where she was on 9/11 and how the city looked.

Cache asked permission to take me upstairs to see her bedroom, but we were told that Mary Ann, her therapist was waiting in her office to meet with us. Cache took me over to the adjacent cabin, which housed a small classroom and four staff offices. I was looking forward to finally meeting Mary Ann, as we had been speaking weekly for months in my phone sessions with Cache. In person, she reinforced my feeling that she and Cache had a good working relationship and that she was right on target with what my daughter needed to work on to move forward in the program and in her therapy.

Then Cache introduced me to her academic teacher, Betsy, whom I had spoken with on the phone a few times when Cache had not done an assignment. It was clear from our phone conversations that Cache's learning disabilities were not being addressed and that she was expected to learn by just paying attention. This approach reminded me of all the bad pre-Stephen Gaynor teaching she had endured. I accepted the fact that Cache might not have the optimum high school education she needed, but that was not why she was here. Then I met Paul, the director of the program. He was a Mormon, as I soon learned were most of the staff. He had a background in special education and deeply believed in the goals and methods he had helped implement at the school. He was probably in his late thirties, with a crew cut and an open midwestern face. He lived nearby with his wife and three young children, with one more on the way. I could see that he genuinely cared about Cache and that she had attached to him as a father figure.

Afterward, we went back to her cabin. She showed me her room, with its two bunk beds, and I met her roommates, Hope, from Oklahoma, and Sasha, from California. They both had similar acting-out backgrounds as Cache, although Hope also had been molested by her grandfather. Then we went downstairs, below the kitchen level, to the family room, where we could have some private time together, as Cache was not allowed to go off-site with me on this first visit. From time to time I heard a girl yell out, "May I go downstairs?" or "May I go upstairs?" and then a wait till a staff member gave the OK. Cache told me their bathroom time was always timed, and their showers could last no longer than three minutes.

She asked me questions about her friends and whether any had called, and how BB was doing without her. I knew it was against the rules, but I discretely called Stu, her god father, on my cell phone for her to say a quick hello and hear his voice wishing her well. Of course this opened the way for her to ask me if we could also call her friend Nina. I knew this would get us both in trouble and made myself say a firm "No" and quickly put my phone back in my bag.

When it was time for dinner, we could join the other girls upstairs or I could drive to the tiny main street nearby and pick up some food for us both. Cache said she was craving Chinese food ever since she saw some parents bring it in on their visit. I'd seen the restaurant, Chin Ming just before I made the turn onto the back road to her school. While I was waiting for my order of chicken and broccoli and cold sesame noodles, I wondered why this Chinese family had settled in this tiny town in the midst of Arizona.

I'd been nervous about the prospect of seeing Cache again after we'd been apart so long, but I felt we connected almost immediately. It was very hard for me to leave her, and I saw that she was having trouble parting from me. I made myself say goodbye at around seven and drove back the few miles to my Comfort Inn room, my mind filled with images of our time together. As I tried to sleep, I kept imagining Cache's life there with the other girls in that cabin and how much more she'd grow and change by our next visit. I comforted myself with the thought that unless she regressed, I would now be able to visit her every month and begin the process of tying our two journeys together.

Secretly, I worried whether I would be able to make any progress in my own journey. I worried that being a mother was so ingrained in my psyche that I had lost any other identity somewhere along the way.

I was no longer that young actress full of ambition and burning with dreams of glowing in the spotlight. I was no longer the writer and jewelry designer, making the rounds of the morning talk shows and creating my jewelry line. I was no longer the rehab counselor, redirecting and giving hope to my disabled patients. Nor was I any longer the medical office manager I had morphed into, or the sort-of paralegal working in my sister's firm. I missed having a creative or even useful goal each day. I needed to find that elusive inner motivating something. All this was on my mind as I flew back to New York….and home.

On Thanksgiving night, as I sat in front of the TV eating my turkey breast and sweet potato, I thought of Cache and the other girls I had met sitting around the table in their cabin having their holiday meal far away from their families. I wondered whether she felt as lonely as I did. Then I made myself remember we had celebrated our Thanksgiving together two weeks earlier.

twenty eight

And miles to go before I sleep

Robert Frost

Almost each month, for the duration of her stay, I got on a plane to Phoenix, rented a car and visited my daughter. In between, we kept in touch with weekly phone sessions and letters.

Her therapy sessions focused on trying to help her heal the wounds left from her early childhood traumas in Guatemala. At one point, Mary Ann called me and said she wanted to try a technique called EMDR. She explained that this was a relatively new technique utilizing right/left eye movement, which, by activating the opposite sides of the brain, helped to release emotional experiences that are trapped in the nervous system. As these troubling images and feelings are processed by the brain via the eye-movement patterns, resolution of the issues is achieved. I called Jeanette, Cache's old therapist in New York, to get her input. She had heard positive feedback about the results from psychiatrists who had used it with trauma patients. And so, with Cache agreeing, I gave the go-ahead.

Cache's Journal

Dear Mom. Right now in therapy I am doing EMDR and so far it's been helping me, although at times I have flashbacks of bad things. The good thing is I don't have to talk about the past. All I do is sit in front of Mary Ann and watch her hand go back and forth. My hair is longer now, way past my shoulders. Sometimes I wear it down in pigtails or a bun or in two buns on top of my head. I can't wait to see you next month.

As time went on, she slowly moved forward through the four levels—with regressions along the way back to a lower level, then forward again a few weeks or sometimes months later. I visited her every month, except when she didn't meet her goals. Then I'd be asked to postpone a visit until she did. It took her seven months to move up to Level Three, which allowed her to go off campus on our visit. I celebrated this big step by taking her to the Hilton Spa Hotel in the nearby town of Sedona, which was set in the midst of exquisite red sandstone mountains. In between exploring the town's art galleries and shops, I treated us both to the hotel's spa massages and manicures. At night we lay in our matching double beds and watched reruns of *Law and Order* and talked about what I did and whom I talked to at home, and how Cache wanted to redo her room when she came home and which restaurants she missed the most. These times together gave me hope that there was a chance my daughter would soon be healed and able to return safely to the real world.

During her time at Copper Canyon, I didn't want her to lose track of her family, sparse as it was. And now that she had moved up to the level of being allowed off campus, I tried to arrange times for her to connect with her sister and her godfather. Debora's mother was caring enough to arrange a trip with Debora to visit a cousin of theirs who lived in nearby Preston, Arizona. In this way Debora was able to spend an afternoon with Cache and even have a therapy session with her. From that time on, they were allowed phone calls as well. Also, Stu and his newest wife, who turned out to be a grown-up and appeared to truly care about Cache, came to visit for a weekend and were able to take her off campus to Sedona, where they were allowed to spend the day with her.

Back home, while Cache was changing her life, I was working on finding "a something" to which I could connect. When I read about a theatre travel club, I joined and spent a week in Canada at the two Shakespeare festivals. Another time I toured the summer theatre circuit in the Berkshires. A friend suggested I try an Olivia cruise to the Bahamas, so I spent a week on a boat with several hundred other lesbians. I felt so emotionally removed from the dating scene that I couldn't get into it, although I met some interesting women with whom I exchanged a few email addresses and then lost track.

In the meantime, Cache continued making progress in her program. As she moved up to each new level of *Achievement* and *Responsibility*, she was required to participate in an Awareness seminar, and I, as her mother, was concurrently required to participate in a Parent seminar. These seminars were three days long and filled with intensive exercises in self- awareness and internal explorations aimed at helping us overcome barriers to reshaping and improving our parent-child relationships. The belief was that "our children did not get to this place by themselves."

My first seminar was in February 2004, about a week after Cache completed her first seminar. I arrived at the Phoenix Airport, picked up my rented car, and drove to the exit just past the one I usually took to visit Cache. As I turned off the highway onto a newly paved brick road, I saw a large sign welcoming visitors to the Yavapai-Apache Casino. Copper Canyon Academy had rented rooms in the motel adjacent to the casino for the parents taking this seminar. After I unpacked my things, I explored the brightly lit and very noisy and bustling casino. I flashed back to a distant memory of myself as a teen peeking into a Las Vegas casino when my parents took me and my sister on a road trip across country. I had been too young then to be allowed in. Now, I walked into a world of bright flashing lights and loud music and the continuous sound of dealers' voices and ringing bells. I saw aisles and aisles jam-packed with people sitting at slot machines with cups full of coins, and an image flashed into my mind of my mother complaining about her sore arm after a day of pulling down slot machine handles.

That night, after I treated myself to a steak dinner in the most elegant of the casino restaurants, I looked around for some other parents but did not see anyone who looked to me like a parent of a troubled teen. I went to my room and read the brochure I had been given to prepare me for the next day. It was titled "*Awakening, a seminar on personal and family development.*" I fell asleep thinking about my daughter and of the personal exploration I was about to embark on to help me help our relationship.

When I walked into the large conference room in the motel lobby, I began to meet the other parents whose daughters had just completed their first seminar along with Cache. There was one divorced mom and eight couples. Over the next three days, I shared all my waking hours with them.

Dear Cache

I am in the midst of my three day seminar. My first thought is how proud I am of you that you were brave enough to take it last week—and I'm awe struck that you did all the work needed to complete it. I was nervous the first day, but as I got to know the other parents I began to feel comfortable and safe with them and with the staff. I heard about the difficult and painful times each of them had gone through with their daughters and the almost unbearable decision they each made sending their daughters to CCA. I feel a bond with them through the love we all have for our daughters and the pain we each endure in keeping them here in this program and we all are going to stay in touch and help each other through the times ahead.

The most powerful exercise we did was a blindfold exercise where I had to visualize and talk to my mother, then my father, and then my inner child. I thought my unresolved issues would be with my mother, but I was surprised to realize I had worked out the need to connect with her during those last three years when she was sick and I was able to care for her and touch her. Instead I was blown away by the emotion I felt when I next visualized my father and felt myself immediately pouring out about how much I had needed him as a child and always felt he was unable to connect with me. As I talked to him in my mind I began to sob and couldn't stop, and then someone, I guess it was one of the staff, knelt down next to me and hugged me while I kept crying for what felt like an eternity. Finally I was able to stop my tears. A voice in my ear told me to relax and move on. I took several deep breaths and although I really didn't believe I had an inner child, I relaxed and allowed myself to imagine talking to the child I remembered being so many years ago, and I was amazed to discover that she was still inside me. She had survived all these years and I felt and saw she was OK.

After the exercise I was given a sheet of paper and a blue magic marker and asked to write anything I wanted. In large letters I wrote "I'M OK." I'm going to take it home and hang it up on my desk bulletin board to remind me, in case I ever forget.

I feel I am taking from the seminar a release from my past sadnesses that will allow me to more fully connect to you and that this will help our relationship heal. When we see each other in two days, I hope you will share with me your seminar experience.

I love you with all my being and am content in my heart that this place, this time, these people are the key to your growth and ability to gain the tools you need to find happiness for yourself at last. I love love you
Mommy

I hadn't thought about my father for several years, but when I went to bed that night in my motel room, after writing to Cache, my mind was filled with memories of his fair-skinned and freckled face, and the thin strands of reddish hair on his prematurely balding head, that Joan and I inherited. I could see him in summer white pants, striped tee shirt, his favorite tan and white shoes, and wearing a straw bowler hat at a dapper angle, looking just like Fred Astaire in one of his movies.

He always walked around with a pipe clenched in his teeth even when it wasn't lit. I remember watching him perform his pipe ritual. First, clearing the old smelly burnt leaves out of the bowl, then opening his tobacco pouch, slowly packing the bowl with new fragrant leaves, and tamping the leaves down in the bowl. Sitting back in his chair, he'd then strike a match and begin the delicate process of lighting the tobacco leaves. Finally the pipe lit, he could relax with his newspaper as he slowly puffed away—sometimes blowing perfect smoke rings for my enjoyment. He also performed this ritual one-handed, while driving the car. As I fell asleep, I remembered the taste of the burnt leaves on my tongue from when he allowed me to pretend to smoke one of his pipes.

twenty nine

I sent Cache to Copper Canyon from the wilderness program in May 2003, just before her thirteenth birthday. For the next two and a half years, I trekked back and forth to visit her and attend parent seminars and workshops and countless therapy sessions together and apart.

During all that time, I knew Cache was completely open to all the staff and all the other girls about the fact that her mother was a lesbian, the same as she had been all her life in any school setting she'd been in—and she was the first to lodge a complaint or speak up whenever anyone said or made jokes about someone's being gay. Whenever she told a fellow student who had been making fun of someone as being gay that her mom was a lesbian, the answer she got was, "Wow. No kidding. But she's so great." The same was true at CCA. In this predominately Mormon setting, there seemed to be a discomfort around the subject, and sometimes open disparagement uttered by a fellow student and at times by a junior staff member working with the girls in their cabin.

I, too, was completely open with staff and requested that the staff member be asked not to express their personal beliefs in the school setting. I had always been open with everyone in my life before then–except my mother, who had somehow sent a silent message to me that she didn't want to know.

But I watched myself surprisingly not discussing my own sexual orientation with any of the parents I became friendly with, nor bringing up the subject in any of our seminars. There was one family I wanted to be open with, as our daughters were close friends and probably would continue as such after CCA. On one visit, we all went out to lunch together at the local Johnny Rocket, a very popular and unique hamburger chain out west.

The husband was a doctor in the midwest whose practice included prayer meetings with his patients. I began to open a discussion of the topic, and he immediately began quoting the Bible, chapter and verse, so I changed the subject to what to order for dessert.

In the two-and-a-half years Cache was at CCA, there was only one girl, who came near the end of Cache's stay who had two mothers. But there were several girls whom Cache told me had questions about their own sexuality, questions which were always brushed aside by staff.

During one of my visits, after Cache had been at CCA almost two years, there was a special group session with parents and our daughters. The parents were seated in a line, our daughters were sitting in a line opposite us, and two staff people were moderating. In that session, the staff encouraged the girls to openly talk about any issue they felt had not been addressed in their time at CCA and that they needed to deal with.

One of the girls raised her hand and began unburdening her heart; "I know I am a lesbian and I have tried to bring up this topic in therapy and in group session, but have always been shrugged off with answers like, "Oh this is probably a phase you are going through or this is something you can change if you really wanted to." By the end of her confession she had begun to cry, and her mother had reached over the aisle to hand her a tissue.

I knew I could not keep silent any longer. As I raised my hand, I glanced over at Cache and winked. I saw in her eyes a look of encouragement to support this girl in her brave step to speak up. I stood, facing the girl and said, "I am a lesbian mother, and anyone who thinks differently should know that being a lesbian is not a choice, just as being a heterosexual is not a choice. This is who I am, and I hope you and your parents can move on from here." There was silence in the room as I looked down the row of parents. Every one of them was sitting there looking downward into their laps. The silence lasted for several seconds, with no other parent making a comment. Then one of the staff asked for another student to present her question, and the topic was changed. At the end of the meeting, the girl came over to thank me, and I gave her the website of the Lesbian Herstory Archives, which I thought would be able to help her connect with a support group near her when she returned home. I also suggested that she or her parents contact me if they wanted to talk further. She did not contact me, nor did her parents.

Finally, in the fall of 2005, even though Cache did not have a graduation date set, I couldn't bear the thought of us being separated any longer, and I initiated the idea of her coming home. From my visits with her and from the reports I got, I felt that enough was enough and it was time for her to come home. The staff at Copper Canyon felt strongly that Cache still needed to be there, that she had not fully internalized the program, and that she still would try to manipulate and bend the rules whenever she could. She had just reached Level Four, and they felt she would need several more months to work on her skills. After that, the process toward graduation required three separate visits home with reduced restrictions each time, then a period of evaluation back at CCA of how the visits went. In addition, Cache would be required to write a home contract relating to her behavior and consequences if she did not follow her contractual obligations. All this could take another four to six months, and even to her sixteenth birthday in June.

I was obsessed with my plan to bring my daughter home and did not listen to how crucial it would be to her growth and development to complete the program; nor did I truly understand how meaningful the graduation process and ritual would be to her. Instead I was focusing on wanting her home to live a normal life, and worrying that she wasn't getting the needed academic courses to graduate or the needed art classes to get into an art program in college.

I thought a safe next step would be a boarding school near home, where she could come home on weekends. I found an all girls boarding school in New Jersey that had a high concentrated in art and design courses and was geared to work with girls who had learning problems. She would be there Monday to Friday and some weekends. So she would just be in the city sporadically, and, I hoped, not reconnect with her old crowd, in particular Bryan, the boy with whom she had run away. I thought this would be the perfect place for her and the perfect entry back into the real world. I pushed the staff to agree with my decision, even enlisting Cache's old therapist, Jeanette, to talk with the CCA staff about follow-up at home. Paul, the director at CCA, and Susanna, Cache's current therapist, reluctantly gave in to my request and arranged an escalated early completion for Cache. She would be allowed to come home for a week's visit in November, after drafting a home visit contract; if that went well, she would have a second visit a month later, and if that went well, she would receive an expedited completion of program.

A staff person drove Cache to the airport in Phoenix, and I met her at La Guardia Airport. I arrived about a half hour early, parked the car, and paced nervously in anticipation for our meeting and her first trip home. She looked so grown-up coming through the gate I almost didn't recognize her, even though I had seen her at school the month before.

She couldn't wait to see her room again, and we talked until late in the night lying on her bed with BB cuddling between us. I thought the home visit went well. Those five days she followed all the rules set up in her contract. We visited The Purnell School in New Jersey and she had a tour and a meeting with the intake person. They loved her and she said she liked the school and wanted to attend.

She flew back to CCA reluctantly, and came home again just before Christmas for her second home visit before her hopeful discharge. On this visit we fine-tuned her home contract and prepared for her to start at Purnell the second week in January.

I believed that when she came home, she would be "cured" and able to make healthy choices in friends and activities, complete high school, go on to college and then a career—and, of course, interact honestly and openly with me—and live happily ever after. At least that was how all the books and memoirs I voraciously read during those two and a half years, had ended.

thirty

When I wake up in the middle of the night, I am sometimes haunted by memories of the biggest mistakes I made in my life, the first being knowing when to stop the doctors from pouring chemo into Julie's body, the second taking Cache home from Copper Canyon Academy before she was ready to graduate, and the third, the decisions I made out of panic and ignorance over the next three years as I sent her from one setting to the next hoping to keep her safe and learn to make healthy choices.

Cache started at Purnell the second week of January 2006, when she was sixteen and a half. She registered for what I thought were courses she would love–ceramics, water color, art history–in addition to the necessary English, Spanish and Biology. When she came home for her first weekend, she told me she hated the school and her opinion did not change during the five months she spent there.

On weekends she returned to sessions with her old therapist, Jeanette, and saw a psychiatrist for her anti-depressant meds. She didn't seem to be any less upset or angry as he fiddled around with dosage and Jeanette continued to talk with her. At this point, her diagnosis was still "depression." Sometimes she connected with old friends or brought a girl from school home for a sleep-over. In an effort to continue healing our relationship, I took her to a Club Med over the Easter vacation. She seemed to enjoy the respite in this setting she had always loved. We spent time together, and I relaxed for the first time in months, lying in the sun, reading, meditating, and walking on the beach.

But I was thrown back into the emerging nightmare when school started up again. I began to get late night phone calls from Cache begging me to take her home, and I would then have to talk her down from her panic before attempting to get some sleep myself. Her panic attacks kept escalating until one night she begged me to put her in a hospital. I called the teacher on duty, who helped her get through the night by inviting her to sleep on the couch in her cabin.

At home on Mother's Day, as we waited for our tiramisu dessert in our favorite Italian restaurant, Cache confided that she had been lying to me and Jeanette and her psychiatrist, that she had been sneaking out at night when she came home and meeting Bryan and some other boys from her past, and that she didn't know how to stop.

I tried to get her back on track by reminding her of her home agreement, with its rules of conduct and rewards and consequences that she swore to follow when she left CCA. She nodded and promised to adhere to her vows and agreed for me to install a dead bolt lock on our front door to help her stay home. On Monday we hugged and she went back to school. But two weekends later, when I woke up Sunday morning and saw her bed empty and the dead bolt lock unscrewed and hanging limply from the wall, I realized once again there was no way I could keep her safe at home.

Cache wanted to be admitted to a hospital, and her psychiatrist recommended the Psych unit at NYU Hospital, where she spent four days lying in bed and having her antidepressant meds changed. As there were no other teens there, her psychiatrist suggested she then spend a few weeks in an adolescent psych program in Westchester. In this new setting, even with others her age she withdrew even more.

So I turned to another consultant, supposedly another "expert," with experience in working with dysfunctional teens. He advised me to send Cache to Wellspring, a small residential program in Connecticut that promised intensive therapy and a new approach. At Wellspring, "attachment disorder" was added to her diagnosis. I had first heard it mentioned at SUWS, then not again. Cache hated this school so much, that after two months, she jumped out of a second-story window late one night and hiked miles along a dark road toward the nearest town, where she thought she could get a ride back to New York; She hoped that when I saw her at our door, I would let her stay.

She was picked up by a police car and taken back to her school. I was called the next morning and immediately drove up. She looked fragile and lost and begged me to take her home. I wanted to cave in but tried to stay strong as I insisted we try to work out a plan for the school to take her back. Then, after she showed she could adhere to the rules, we'd talk about when she could leave. In the meeting with the school head and her counselor, she was told they would take her back only if she agreed to a stringent "shadow program," which included not closing the bathroom door. She looked shocked at this condition and walked out of the meeting. I met her outside and saw in her face that she would only try to leave again. I agreed to take her home on the condition that we would find a program she could accept.

I thought the best next step was to go back to a wilderness program to help her get back on a positive track, remembering how much she had liked the first one and her feeling of accomplishment.

So again, like a worn record, I sent her away. I Googled another SUWS program, this one closer to home, in North Carolina. Four weeks later, I found myself at another graduation ceremony. Afterward Cache cooked dinner around a campfire she again had miraculously created. And once more I spent the night in a sleeping bag in a tent with my daughter. I was surprised to find I enjoyed my camping experience this time around.

I was still fixated on her need to complete high school and enrolled her in the Family School in the upper Catskills. It had a strong high-school agenda in addition to what I was told was a good record for helping adolescents with addictive behavior—drugs, alcohol, and sex —based on a 12-step program. Also, it was a co-ed school, which immediately sold her, and I thought it a good idea for her to finally be in a supervised setting with boys.

At first Cache seemed to like the school and her classmates and her therapist. I drove up to visit every few weekends and sit in on a therapy session with her, which seemed to be going well. Cache's sister, Debora, who had begun taking courses at Ohio State in graphic design, accepted my invitation to come to New York on one of her school holidays, so she could accompany me upstate to visit with Cache. Her brother, Michael, was now in his first year at Annapolis. On another weekend, his family drove him up to meet me at Cache's school so he could spend the afternoon with her while we went to the local Italian restaurant. Afterwards, Cache told me how all the girls had gone "gaga" over her handsome brother.

After Cache had been at Family School for about six months, she began to hate the school and the program and all the teachers. She started begging me to take her home. A month after she turned eighteen, she ran away from the school. I received a phone call telling me she had walked out of the school gates and was on a back road to the nearby town of Hancock. Since she was eighteen, I was told she could not be forced to return to the school. I was advised to let her go, to let her fend for herself without any money or place to go. And again, I couldn't. I kept thinking of what horrors could happen to her on a highway alone with night approaching. I implored the staff person to drive out to where she was and tell her that if she came back with them, I would drive up the next morning and talk with her about alternate plans.

When I drove up the next morning, Cache begged me to take her home, and I agreed one more time–the last time, I told her—but only if she agreed to go to a school I found, which would help her, after all these years in residential settings, to learn how to live in the outside world.

When I look back over all those lost years, I realize except for Copper Canyon and the two wilderness programs, none of the other placements helped–no school, no medication, no therapy. The only thing they did was keep her safe from bodily harm and pregnancy, and me from having to deal with those worries on a daily basis. But worse, all that time away from home and apart from each other, created a deep, deep chasm in our mother daughter relationship.

thirty one

2007

I read and reread the blurb for Milestones for Young Adults on the web after it was recommended by our newest educational consultant. It promised to be the place where young adults eighteen to twenty-four who have had troubled childhoods and been in therapeutic programs through most of their teens would have a safe environment to learn the skills they needed to live independently in the outside world. "Exactly what Cache needs," I thought. "Amazing, there seems to be a program for every situation."

The downside was that it was located all the way across the country in Coeur d'Alene, Idaho. The only upside was that I could use all those miles I had accumulated going back and forth to CCA and the wilderness programs.

Milestones was different from Cache's past placements. She had her own room and bath in an apartment with two other girls, with whom she shared the kitchen and living room. As in her past programs, there were goals she needed to master before moving ahead to more independence; in the first level she was under strict supervision, and required to participate in peer support groups with mentoring, while learning to shop, cook, budget, and gain experience doing volunteer work. In the second level she could make the transition to a college, or trade school, or work experience. The third level would give her more and more freedom in choosing outside unsupervised activities, including learning to drive. In the fourth level she would begin actual independent living with a life-coach support in place. She was seeing a psychiatrist as part of the program, and now her diagnosis changed to bipolar with a possibility of borderline personality.

I couldn't understand why Cache did not progress quickly toward these tantalizing rewards, but the only obligation she was fulfilling was attending and participating in the group rap and therapy sessions. After six months, the only progress she had made was to take and easily pass the high school equivalency exam, which she needed in order to register in a cosmetology school. She had always liked to work with makeup and hair styling, and fortunately there was a top rated school right there in Coeur d'Alene. In spite of her still being on level one when the cosmetology school term began the first week of January, the decision was made to allow her to begin the program, in the hope that this would give her the incentive to make more progress toward her independence.

I sat at home the morning of January 8 with my fingers crossed. At noon-time I got a call from Pam, her program's director, telling me how Cache got herself up that morning, bravely swallowed her fears, and had just been driven to her first day of school at Headmasters. Cache's phone call, a few days later, was filled with love for the school and mention of the friends she was making. She explained in depth the various hair styles and braiding she was doing on a mannequin head and was even taking pictures of her styling. I hung up with a sigh of relief and tried to make myself believe all would be fine from now on. It felt so good to be able to relax at night, knowing my daughter was safe and at long last doing something she loved.

Then in the middle of the second week the phone rang at ten in the evening.

"Hi Leni, This is Pam—"

My breath stopped somewhere in my throat and I felt dizzy. I sat down at my desk. "Oh My God, what happened?"

"Last night Cache snuck out around midnight. She stuffed things under her sheets to look like she was there. So far she hasn't come back."

The familiar hysteria started rising in my chest as I fought to take deep breaths and think clearly. This wasn't supposed to happen again. But there was nothing the school could do as she was eighteen, and more important, nothing I would want them to do. I had rescued her three times before. I knew that this time she had to do it herself.

With this decision, I felt a kind of peace that I had not experienced in the past. I used to eat myself up worrying and expend enormous energy, thinking that my words carried the strength to influence her actions. It finally dawned on me: I couldn't make things better anymore. I had to accept that she needed to find that strength in herself. What made it a bit easier was that Coeur d'Alene was a small town, and the program assured me they were keeping track of Cache's activities: of the few days she did go to her school, where she was staying, and of the boy she was with. Thinking that Cache was not in as much danger in this little resort town as she would have been on the streets of Manhattan or on a dark highway in upstate New York helped me keep my resolve.

Two weeks later, the phone rang. It was a young man from Cache's cosmetology school named Roy. He told me he had picked Cache up from her boyfriend's apartment, where she was no longer allowed to stay, as his father had laid down the law that he was not going to support his son and a girlfriend as well. Jay said he had just driven her to the women's shelter.

Then I got an email.

Dear Mom

 I know you are probably mad and disappointed with me. And I'm really sorry. I just couldn't do it anymore and also I didn't really want to either. I know I have made a mess of my life and that you probably feel like I have spit in your face. I am so sorry! I know I can't come home. I'm not asking you to. And I'm not asking for your money or your help either. I know I blew that too. I do want to stay in contact with you and see you whenever you are ready to see me if you ever are. I want you to know that I am OK and that I have found a few safe places to stay with people who are willing and are going to help me. I love you mom. I know I have been stupid the last month or so. I just hope that my stupidity doesn't cause me to completely lose you.
Again I love you and will e-mail you sometime soon.
Love Cache

I read it over and over, taking in each word and accepting her decision, as hard as that was for me, and as worried I was that she was not yet prepared to be on her own.

Finally I emailed her back.

Dear Cache

 My only wish is that you find happiness and peace in your life. I am not angry with you. I am just sad, very sad that you make life so difficult for yourself. I am sorry that the way you deal with things is to leave in the middle and run away.

Hopefully you will be able to work things thru in a better way in the future…..

I would like very much to know what your plans are. I believe you owe me that. I hope you continue to take your meds, as we don't know how much worse you might feel if you stopped. If you ever want to explore alternative meds/ or treatment I would of course help you with that. I look forward to talking with you soon.

All my love now and forever
MOM

thirty two

Your little voice over the wires came leaping

e.e.cummings

A week later, at eight on Monday night, I got a call from Cache. She was in Sioux City, South Dakota. "Hi Mom, I'm sorry. I couldn't do it anymore. Don't worry, I'm safe now. I'm on a Greyhound bus going to Ohio to stay with Debora at her college, and Michael even sent her some money to help pay my expenses."

When I heard this I was filled with fury that her sister was rescuing her from what she had gotten herself into, and at the same time, with relief that she was being saved from what she had gotten herself into and was now going to a safe place.

The next call came late Tuesday night from Minneapolis. Her bus was late and missed its connecting bus to Chicago, so they all were camping out in the bus depot overnight till the Wednesday morning bus to Chicago got there. It sounded as if she had bonded with a family who were traveling cross country and a young man who was on his way to meet up with his fiancée somewhere along that bus's route. She sounded very tired as she told me she had run out of money for food and was depending on whatever fellow passengers offered her. I heard from her next almost a day later, when she reached Chicago and was boarding the bus that would take her to Toledo, her final destination. That's where Debora was going to meet her and drive her to the apartment she shared with three other girls, and where Debora thought she was going to teach her how to live in the real world after I had secluded her from reality for so many years.

During these four days I lived in limbo, always staying in reach of a phone and with my cell phone on whenever I went out. After each call, I plotted Cache's long four-day trek across the country on a map I pinned up on my bulletin board next to the phone. A few times a day I made myself eat, searching the refrigerator for something that appealed to me but having no appetite.

I kept calling the Greyhound terminal in Toledo, trying to get an accurate arrival time for Debora to be there, emailing and calling Debora with new info as I got it. I also spoke with Ila, Debora's mother, home in Iowa, who was horrified with the news her daughter had taken on such a huge and potentially difficult task. I felt helpless, which is not a way I like to feel. Everything was out of my control, and no one knew better than I how unprepared Cache was for this transition into the real world.

What high hopes I had when I brought her home from Copper Canyon two years ago; and when I found the perfect transition setting for her at Purnell, where I imagined she'd finish high school as she immersed herself in art classes and prepared for college. Then came the Wellspring School disaster followed by the Family School disaster. And now that she had rejected Milestones so dramatically by choosing a woman's shelter, how could I believe she would succeed this time?

But—this was the sister, who along with her brother, had taken care of her as a young child, shielding her as best they could from the abuse of their birth mother. If this didn't work out, would Cache ever be able to live independently or would she always need to be in a sheltered environment? And how would she accept that alternative?

Her bus finally arrived in the Toledo terminal late Thursday afternoon. Debora was there to pick her up and drive her to her apartment. I got an email from Debora telling me all was well and that she was going to give Cache a few days to get herself together and then she would help her find a job. I didn't hear from either of them until around ten on Saturday night.

When I picked up the phone Cache was on the other end crying. "Mom please come and get me. Please let me come home. Debora just beat me up and I'm scared to stay here any longer."

"Wait a minute, Cash, go slowly. Tell me what happened."

"I went to a party with her and her roommates Thursday night and we all got drunk. Then Friday night she left me in the apartment with one of her roommates and didn't come back till Saturday afternoon. And a little while ago, I was sitting on the bed with my computer and she came over to me and started beating me up."

"Where is she now?"

"She's sitting in front of the door so I can't leave. I was going to leave. There's a boy I met in a store in Idaho after I ran away from Milestones. I just IM'd him and he said he would send me a ticket to come to him in Oklahoma."

"What? Cache, are you crazy? How could you think of doing that? You don't even know this guy. You don't know what you would be getting into. Let me talk to Debora."

I heard Cache tell Debora to get on the phone. Then I heard Debora's strained voice say hello.

"Debora, tell me what is happening."

"I am guarding the door so Cache can't leave."

"She said you beat her up. Did you beat her up?"

"Yes"

"Why, what happened?"

"I don't know. When she told me she was going to leave here and go off with a boy she didn't even know, I just lost it. Sometimes when I'm drunk, I get so angry I can't control myself, I don't know why. I promised Cache I won't do it again, I won't drink any more. I just want to take care of her."

While I was hearing this barrage of emotion and scary events, I was figuring out what to do. All the warnings from all the programs I had sent my daughter to kept echoing in my head that I should not, and I could not, rescue her. I was supposed to let her go.

When Cache came back on the phone I knew I couldn't do what I was supposed to do. So I gave up my brief enrollment in the tough love club and decided to bring my wounded daughter home. I heard myself tell her I would take her home, but she had to promise me she'd follow the rules of the house. She immediately agreed and begged me to make a plane reservation for her that night. Over her objections, I told her nothing could be done that late and that I would call her the next day after I made bus reservations for her to come to the Port Authority, where I would pick her up. Her voice sounded exhausted as she thanked me. I gently said "Try and sleep and we'll work everything out in the morning." I spoke with Debora again saying I would call in the morning, and I got her to promise to take Cache to the terminal if she still wanted to come home. Then I hung up, completely exhausted, and sick with fears about what lay in store when Cache came home; and would I be able to handle it?

thirty three

And there I will keep you forever,
Yes, forever and a day,
Till the wall shall crumble to ruin,
And molder in dust away

H.W. Longfellow

Debora tried to convince Cache to stay in Ohio with her but finally drove her to the Greyhound bus terminal Sunday morning to catch the bus to Manhattan. I again glued my attention to the map on my wall and continued to plot my daughter's journey across the country.

Cache called me Sunday night from the Pittsburgh terminal, where she had to change buses. She asked me where to get off the bus when it got to New York and where I would meet her. I was reminded how inexperienced travel-wise she was after spending all her teen years in sheltered settings.

I kept imagining her sitting on that bus through the night as she made her way home to me. I wondered what plans she was hatching in her head, whom she would reconnect with, what control or influence would I have, if any, now that she was eighteen. That night, I Cache-proofed the apartment, moving the bottle of vodka from the freezer and the six bottles of wine that had just arrived from a wine club I joined on the web from the linen closet to a friend's apartment down the hall. We never knew if Cache had a problem with drinking because she had been in programs all these years, but from the stories she related about drinking to excess each time there was liquor available when she had gone to parties at home or when she ran away, she thought that maybe she did have an addiction. I also made sure there was no money lying around as temptation, just in case she decided to run again. I continued to have no appetite, as usual when I was anxious, but forced myself to eat anyway. I reverted to the comfort foods from before my conversion to the South Beach low carb diet and my resulting flat tummy. My mother's mashed potatoes fried with eggs went down easily, as did Terri's buttery version of cinnamon toast. I made a list of everything I expected Cache to abide by and the consequences that would apply if she didn't follow the rules of living at home. This had not worked for long in her past returns home, but I was hoping this time she would follow them. All the while, preparing to make myself let her go if she didn't.

I couldn't sleep and spent much of the night surfing the channels to keep my mind off what lay ahead. I kept busy Monday morning, making Cache's bed with her favorite quilt and then shopping at Fairway for foods I thought she might enjoy: macaroni and cheese, ramen soup, chocolate chip cookies, mangos, kiwis. I finally couldn't stay home any longer and left early to pick her up, taking a book for while I waited. But Cache's bus had already arrived. When I got to her gate, there she was, sitting on a bench reading a fashion magazine, her feet up on a duffle bag that Debora must have given her, leaning against the stuffed overnight bag that she had been allowed to take with her from Milestones. I was greeted with a big smile and a very tight hug, which felt so good. Hand in hand, we made our way down the escalator and into one of the cabs lined up outside that seemed to be waiting to take me and my daughter home.

As we entered our lobby, Cache was greeted with, "Hello, great to see you again," from our doorman and our elevator operator. Some of my friends called to welcome her home, but she always was sleeping. In fact, the first few days Cache slept almost round the clock. Then she started waking around four in the afternoon and staying up all night on the couch watching TV while on her computer, IMing for hours and hours. Then she'd fall asleep again around five in the morning and sleep till four in the afternoon– repeating the cycle all over again.

While she was sleeping, I tried to stay sane by going to my exercise classes and my writing class, having lunch with friends, even going to a movie one afternoon. But my main focus was on making calls to various recommended psychologists and psychiatrists, trying to find the right one who could help my daughter. With each, I shared the list of diagnosis she had acquired as she made her way from one program's psychiatrist to the next. Each diagnosis had sounded like a reasonable explanation at the time for her behavior. What I was looking for now was the definitive expert to finally put all this history together and give me a clear answer to what was wrong with my daughter and how to fix it for good.

I was clear with Cache that she had to see a psychiatrist for medication, and that she needed to also be seeing a therapist, to help her adjust to home and get on the right track to functioning in the real world. In between sleeping, she agreed to this plan, as long as it wasn't a full-time program and I promised not to send her away again.

Finally, I was given the name of a psychiatrist who was the expert's expert in diagnosing bipolar and personality disorders, which were two of the scary choices tossed around by previous experts, along with reactive attachment disorder and the ever-present depression label. I had recited this list in each call I made, along with Cache's recent history. One therapist would recommend another, who would recommend another, as each either did not have time or felt she was not the right one, or was someone I didn't feel good about. Then a therapist said, "The first thing I would do if she were my child would be to get a definitive diagnosis from Dr. Joel Goldberg."

I was pulled in with "if this were my child." I Googled Joel Goldberg and was very impressed with his credentials. I called him and continued to be impressed with his humanity and caring. I made an appointment to drive to Norwalk, Connecticut, for him to diagnose Cache. On the day of the appointment, I spent almost an hour and all my energy trying to wake Cache, using threats and promises, until she got up and dressed and we were on our way.

It was an unusually warm and sunny March day, and I enjoyed driving along the scenic Hutchinson River Parkway as Cache slept beside me. At one point she woke up, looked at me with resignation, and asked whether we were really going to see a new psychiatrist or was I taking her away to another program? Her saying this felt like a knife stabbing me in my heart. How did we arrive at this point of distrust?

An hour later, I pulled up in front of Dr. Goldberg's office. He was a soft-spoken, slightly chubby, middle-aged, sweet mensch who asked the most specific and minute questions of Cache, diagramming her answers on a board in various colored pens while developing for us the clearest picture and understanding of what he believed her problems were and what needed to be done.

First, he concluded that Cache was not bipolar in any of its various manifestations. She was, however, clearly in a major depression, and from her answers had been so for most of her teen years, in spite of the anti-depression meds she had been on. He suggested raising her Prozac a bit to see if that would help and said that in time he might add other meds if that wasn't enough to give her relief. He also impressed on her the need for her to reverse her sleep pattern and to begin a specific form of cognitive therapy called DBT (Dialectic Behavioral Therapy), developed for use with borderline personality disorders but that he felt would be helpful to her, as it utilized exercises that would systematically help pull her into a more functioning state.

I asked him for a diagnosis. He felt she didn't fit into any specific DSM category other than "depression/unspecified w/ conduct disorder s/p trauma." He also mentioned that she had issues around identity. He did not believe she was emerging as a borderline personality as had the last psychiatrist in Idaho. Rather, he explained to her how the severe abuse in her early years led to her brain's not developing normally, and why this made it difficult for her to cope emotionally as she grew older and caused her to act out impulsively when faced with extreme upset or anger. He likened her behavior to a primitive fight or flight response. This explanation of her uncontrolled past behaviors helped Cache feel less like a failure or a bad person. I could see that his understanding and explaining clearly what she was going through took away her feelings of hopelessness, and for the first time in a long while she felt there was a chance she could and would find some relief.

She agreed to try to change her sleep pattern, and over the next month, with my consistent direction, she began to reverse it. For a few weeks, every day I was in battle with her to wake up and every night I was in battle with her to go to sleep. On the plus side, for the first time in all the times she had come home between programs, she did not run away or even go out in the middle of the night. In fact, one night she woke me up, saying, "Mom, I felt like running but I don't want to." I pulled back the covers and she crawled into bed next to me and BB. We talked a bit as I rubbed her back till she fell asleep. This was a first.

I found a therapist just a few blocks away who practiced DBT. Arielle was willing to see Cache once a week, with the hope of adding a group session as time went on. Arielle looked like a young Julia Roberts as she leaned forward, pushing her hair back from her face, making her points to Cache. Cache connected with her right away and told me she really felt she had someone on her side.

With the structure Arielle was now providing for Cache, she began to think about going back to school. We looked on the web at the cosmetology schools in the city, and her eyes lit up as she read the details of the two schools that focused on makeup rather that the broad range of disciplines—hair, nails and makeup. I made appointments for us to tour them. When we walked into the second school, Cache made an immediate connection with Lia, the director, an elegantly dressed and coiffed older woman with a soft Israeli accent. She told us she had raised a daughter as a single mom as well. After giving Cache a tour of the school, she took her hand and said, "I will treat you as my daughter. You are going to have a great time here and learn how to be the makeup artist that you want to be." The wheels were set in motion for Cache to begin classes the next week.

I had the familiar butterflies in my stomach Monday morning when my alarm went off at eight, so I could help Cache get moving on this her first day. I truly did not know if she would go or not. I kept repeating, like a mantra, "Let it go. You can't do it for her. Cache has to do it herself."

And she did get up and go to her new school, some days more reluctantly than others. But each day taking steps that would lead her toward self-sufficiency, and, I hoped, fulfillment.

thirty four

Love's the I guess most only verb that lives

e.e.cummings

It took Cache almost a year to complete the six-month course at the Lia Schoor Institute of Skin Care Training. After the first few weeks, she began to miss classes and avoid tests, but with my exhausting insistence she finally did complete the program. The teachers all kept working with her and encouraging her, as they saw her talent and skills in this field. The next step was taking the New York State certifying exam, so she would have the credentials to work as a makeup artist. It took her two months to register for the written part of the exam, and another two for the practical. About a month later she received an envelope from the New York State Department of Labor with her license to work as a *Makeup Artist and Esthetician in New York State*.

Looking for a job was another story. There were months of delays and excuses while Cache continued to baby sit, and then a burst of effort, and voila—a first job that turned out to be more of a cashier and shelf-filler than a makeup position. A few months later, after a bit more effort, she landed the perfect job, as a makeup and facial consultant and sales person in Sephora, the store of her dreams. She saw this as her first step in her career as a make-up artist. She even began thinking ahead to moving on to working for a cosmetic company and someday doing makeup for a fashion magazine. One day at a time, I keep telling myself.

Cache keeps track, via Facebook, with about 400 kids with whom she was in various programs. Of those, she has seen almost half slip back into their old behaviors after leaving or graduating from the program that was supposed to change their lives. She shared these numbers with me and sees herself as one of those who did benefit and who did change, especially from her time at Copper Canyon.

As I watched her happy face, applying her makeup each morning for work, I remember the times I wanted to throw in the towel, then watched her pull herself together and bravely take a tiny step forward. I know now that whenever she gets angry at me, she is really angry at herself for slipping into old behavior. A few weeks ago, after she had a problem at work, I watched her begin to doubt herself and turn on me, and my stomach clutched with the familiar, "Oh no, not again." As I got ready to fall into bed that night I saw an envelope on my pillow with "MOM" written in capital letters. Inside, in her meticulous hand-writing, on a lined page torn from a spiral notebook, was a letter.

Dear Mom;

I know you are sad and disappointed in me right now. And in some ways I am too, and I am trying to get help. But this isn't what this letter is about. This letter is to thank you. Thank you for never giving up on me. Thank you for doing your best for me all the time. I have spent the last few weeks hearing and seeing and also dealing with parents of friends and children that I babysit for. The things I have seen and heard have shocked me. Some of it I can't even believe. And the reason it shocked me and even scared me is because I know I could have ended up with parents like that. But I didn't. I got you. You who I know no matter what I do will never give up on me. You who spent lots of time, money and energy to always do and find the best for me and will continue to do so.

Thank you for finding Stephen Gaynor. Thank you for sending me to Copper Canyon. Thank you for sending me to Wilderness. And believe it or not, thank you for leaving me homeless in Idaho because it made me grow up. And then, thank you for letting me come home.

Thank you for finding Arielle. Thank you for pushing me to finish at Lia Schoor. I know it wasn't easy for you to try to get me to go each day. Thank you

for always forgiving me when I have hurt you, as I know I have. Thank you for
putting up with my bullshit now and the bullshit that is still to come. Thank
you for giving me the best family anyone could have. Thank you for being you.
THANK YOU FOR BEING MY MOM.
And most of all thank you for loving me. I love you
Love Cache

I was fifty-four years old when I started my search to adopt a child. I still felt young and ready to begin my new adventure in parenting. After all, Jane Fonda had just turned fifty and that fifty was being hyped as the new forty. Once Cache became part of my family and she began to tell me tales of her abuse in Guatemala, I was able to put aside, for good, my buried guilt about what her mother might have felt giving her child away for a TV set.

I knew I made the right choice in adopting her just as I knew I made the right choice when I ignored all those doctors attempts urging me put Julie in a home so "you can move on with your life."

Now that I'm in my seventies (which I am hoping is the new sixties), I feel a particular urgency in helping my daughter move forward in caring for herself and having a career, especially in a job that might give her the satisfaction I felt, first as an actress, then as rehab counselor.

Some days, I feel panic setting in as time rushes by and I have not finished my job with Cache. Then I remember the lesson I learned when I was told Julie had only six months to live. I remember how I woke up each morning and spent every minute of every day savoring that moment in time we had together. How beautiful each flower looked, how delicious each meal tasted, how special was each conversation we had. That was the gift Julie gave me, and I need to keep that lesson alive as I wake up each day now, with Cache needing my support as she struggles to make her way toward a healthy life.

I don't know when that will happen.

I don't know how many back and forths there will be.

But I do know that as long as I'm breathing, I'll be here for my daughter.

Coda

I have written a great deal about the steps I took toward helping my daughter reach a healthy point in her life. What I have discovered, as I relived those decisive moments, is that some decisions I made were not in the best interest of my child—and perhaps not any child.

I know there is a very fine line between a child's not benefiting from a program because that child did not adhere to the program or sabotaged themselves: and the possibility that the program was indeed a bogus program with a staff ill-trained and ill-suited to employ the appropriate therapeutic methods needed to benefit a participant.

Now, after the fact, I am aware that one of the schools I sent Cache to was at one point under investigation for improper treatment of students; another I believe should have be investigated for hiring unqualified staff.

Most of the decisions I made along the way were made with the help and guidance of so- called professionals in the field of child and adolescent therapy, people whom a parent would expect to have the appropriate knowledge to make an informed decision about a program they were recommending.

In retrospect, I have come to realize that some of the "professionals" I relied upon were not experts; or had not investigated the validity of the practices, programs or methodology utilized by the so-called therapeutic institutions they recommended; or, in some cases, had not investigated the credentials of the staff itself.

On one hand, I can't ignore the real possibility that my daughter might not be alive today if I had not intervened. But I also can not negate the damage done by isolating her from "real life" from age thirteen and a half to almost nineteen; with the result that she lived her entire teen age years away from home and family, a factor that has handicapped her in ways from which she may never recover. Most notably, it denied her the opportunity to test her abilities to make friends outside her therapeutic settings, and to learn to trust her instincts in unstructured real-life situations.

During the last few years I watched as Cache and her sister Debora took the first steps toward reconciliation as they began to speak to each other via facebook and texting. And last year when Michael brought them together as part of his wedding celebration, I watched the three of them and knew in my heart that they were again a family.

Even though Cache has been home for two years, and has had the opportunity to meet new people and try new activities, I watch her struggle daily with who she is and what she deserves in life. I continue to hope that one day she will be able to tap into the potential I know she has.

Thanks to

The late Carol Lane, my first writing teacher at the 92nd Street Y. for helping me explore my life's history and begin to put it on paper. And to the other women in my class who listened and accepted my stories and who so bravely shared their amazing stories with me.

My dear friend Joan Nestle, who was there in the beginning sifting through all my writing, asking me the right questions to dig deeper into the stories I had inside me and needed to tell. And to Melody Lawrence for reinforcing in me the feeling that my story was worth telling and directing me toward a more focused exploration of that story.

I have deep gratitude to Patty Dann and my fellow writers, Phyllis Dolgin, Beth Rosen, Lenore Migdal, Rochelle Rosenbaum and Rebecca Painter who sat around the table with me in Patty's writing workshop, giving me courage to keep going as I shaped the emerging story of a young woman becoming a mother and facing life's impossible choices. And also to Vivian Conan who read my work with great care as she edited and suggested cuts which kept the story moving without losing my essence. And to my friend Susan Black who came to the rescue and performed magic whenever my computer decided to play tricks on me; and who along with Susan Matthias helped me make those last critical artistic decisions about layout and design.

Thanks also to Glenn Doman and the IAHP staff who, against the tirades from traditional medical establishment, created and taught a controversial method of physical therapy to parents in search of a way to help their disabled child live a better life… and which did succeed in giving Julie twenty years of an improved life. The need for volunteers to carry out this rigorous program created the miracle of bringing into our lives a multitude of people answering a sign to "come for an hour a week to help exercise a disabled young girl." The bond of friendship created by working together toward this common goal has lived on with many of our "patterners" staying connected and becoming dearest friends and extended family.

Cache and I also want to say thanks to The Stephan Gaynor School and its dedicated staff and teachers who exuded positive vibes and turned her heavy burden of learning into the joy of learning. Special thanks to the SUWS Wilderness Programs in Idaho and in North Carolina… and to Copper Canyon Academy in Arizona, under the supervision of Paul Taylor, for creating the programs which helped Cache emotionally survive and grow toward a healthy and safer maturity, while also guiding me toward becoming a better mother.

And lastly. I want to express my deepest love and gratitude to my daughter Cache, who so bravely allowed me to read and then incorporate her amazing journal entries and letters into this memoir, which add an illuminating extra dimension to the story of our family.

About the Authors

Leni Goodman spent the first half of her life as a working actress in TV, films and on the stage in summer stock and Off Broadway. She then moved on to a career as a psychological counselor before turning to writing. Her first work was a craft book "Art From Shells" for Crown Publishers, which she co-wrote with her then husband. Now she has turned her writing efforts to her life's story, journeying from young woman and wife to the joy of becoming a mother... little knowing the nightmares and impossible choices ahead.... or the inner strength she would need to face and overcome the challenges presented to her. She hopes that her story will be of help to others, especially parents, who may find themselves facing adversities.

Cache Goodman is a talented artist and writer ... and brave survivor of her traumatic first years. She continues to work in overcoming her early legacy as she moves forward toward a happy and fulfilling life. She now has the credentials and skills as a Make-up Artist and Esthetician. Also, her recent adoption of a stray boxer/pit bull puppy she named Destiny has opened new possibilities for her in the field of dog training and care.

Made in the USA
Lexington, KY
02 December 2016